Marion Merrick

NOW YOU SEE IT, NOW YOU DON'T

SEVEN YEARS IN HUNGARY
1982-1989

Copyright Mágus Publishing Ltd.

First published 1998 by
MÁGUS PUBLISHING LTD

Edited by Peter Doherty 1999.

MARION MERRICK

NOW YOU SEE IT, NOW YOU DON'T

SEVEN YEARS IN HUNGARY
1982-1989

For Miklós who showed us the 'real' Hungary;

for Paul without whose encouragement I would never have started to write;

for John and Hannah - to show why we stayed.

★

With many thanks to Imre Szász, Dr Éva Bán, Zoli Gráf, Péter Simon, Ben Lasserson and Anne Martin for the various ways they helped me during the writing of this book; and to Peter Doherty for his blue-pencil work!

Introduction

Hungary, some 1200 miles from England, may not seem like a very adventurous place to think of spending a year. But the year was 1982, and the country was still behind the iron curtain. There were, in fact, no more than a dozen British people resident in Budapest, none of whom we knew.

If true life is said to be always stranger than fiction then the string of coincidences which led us to this journey readily supports the theory. In 1977, we were newly-married and struggling to survive on my undergraduate grant in Sheffield. Paul had begun his Ph.D. on the composer Liszt but had no funding, and his attention had been drawn to a British Council Scholarship to study for two months abroad. Paul carefully considered the merits of both Weimar in East Germany, and Budapest, but finally decided on the latter. He duly filled in the forms, exaggerating his prowess in various languages, especially Hungarian – he had just learnt to count to ten.

In the intervening weeks before we heard that Paul was being summoned for interview, he lost some of his original enthusiasm for the trip. However, the letter of invitation to the interview stated that travelling expenses to London would be covered, and this decided us.

At Christmas we travelled to Germany with my mother to see her sister and arrived back early in January. There, among the late Christmas cards and bills, lay an envelope from the British Council: Paul's date of departure was to be January 31st. The short letter ended with the words, 'We hope someone will meet you at the station in Budapest. As yet we have no further details.'

Paul arrived at Budapest's Keleti (eastern) Station on February 1st, 1978, in snow and temperatures well below zero, armed with his booklet from the British Council entitled 'Advice for Visitors to Communist Countries'. This included warnings on everything from getting involved in compromising situations with people likely to lure or blackmail you into working for the KGB, to hidden microphones in flowerpots of hotel rooms or rented accommodation. He was soon approached by a Hungarian wearing a sheepskin coat, fur hat, and with a leather bag slung over one shoulder, who spoke good, if hesitant English. This was Miklós, who taught at the Karl Marx University of Economics and had received a telephone call in the middle of a lesson that morning from the Ministry of Culture, where he did odd interpreting jobs. He was asked to meet an English musician arriving on the Vienna train.

'But how will I recognise him?' Miklós had asked.

'Oh, easy,' came the reply. 'He looks typically English.'

Miklós was officially only employed for three days but a friendship developed, and the two of them met almost daily throughout Paul's two-month stay. Following this visit, Miklós came to England where we met again, and we visited Hungary in 1980 and 1981. Without realising it, we had fallen in love with the country, and formed new, deep friendships. Somehow, when the possibility of spending a year in Budapest was suggested by someone at the Music Academy it seemed too good a chance to miss. Thus, in July 1982 leaving just cat and piano behind, we set off for Budapest.

*

When deliberating on how to organise, write and present the episodes in this book, I spoke to my brother who offered this simple piece of advice: 'Just tell it how it was.'

None of the characters, places or events that follow are in any way fictitious. This is *exactly* how it was…

While I have tried to avoid using too many Hungarian words, some were unavoidable.

néni – aunty } terms of respect used by children to address
bácsi – uncle} adults, or by adults for elderly people.

Others will be explained in the story as we go along.

Beginnings and Belongings
VÁNTUS KÁROLY STREET

We had arrived. Rákóczi Square – a square with a huge covered market and stalls spilling on to the pavement, grubby children playing in a fenced-off area, old men engrossed in chess under straggling trees and on the corner, two girls loitering and smoking – the regulars, who have made the name of Rákóczi Square synonymous with prostitution. A tram rattled past along the dusty boulevard, an inner ring road which crosses the Danube by way of two bridges. Everything was hot, parched, dusty and noisy.

It seemed somehow appropriate that Miklós should have moved to this infamous square. Miklós, the great observer of people and life, our first friend in Hungary and the one ultimately responsible for our impulsive decision to leave England for a year or two to try our luck in Budapest.

Leaving our VW Beetle bulging with our belongings and the bags of fruit we had bought en route, we walked slowly across the road and into the dark, dirty stone entrance, past the black dustbins and rusty wall-mounted letter-boxes and on up the cool stairway. We had to grope to find the iron banister as coming from the glare of the midday sun we could see nothing at all. Two flights up, a door led out onto an open walkway around the four sides of the courtyard. Most buildings follow this design, some of the courtyards having trees and flowers, even vines, others just dark, empty, concrete yards. What was most striking about this one was the mass of wooden scaffolding from ground to roof level, which Miklós later explained was all that prevented this crumbling block from collapsing.

We rang the bell and Miklós and his wife, Rézi, greeted us with the customary kiss on both cheeks, much laughter and with hugs. They led us into their spacious, airy flat which had twelve-foot high ceilings and parquet floors, in common with most old buildings in the city.

7

We inelegantly flopped on to the armchairs, with our arms and legs spread to cool ourselves. The huge stained-glass windows overlooking the square formed an extraordinary mural of parrots and palm trees, bookcases reached almost to the ceiling on every wall and in a corner stood the traditional *kályha*, a tiled gas-fired stove, which would once have been wood-burning, some seven feet tall. Magazines, newspapers, language textbooks (Miklós taught English and Rézi Russian), cigarette packets, coins and a bowl of fruit covered the small table, around which more papers and scribbled notes had fallen to the floor and spread themselves over to the telephone by the wall adjoining the bedroom.

"Welcome behind the iron curtain!' Miklós smiled. 'Now, what would you like to drink? Brandy, whisky?' Rézi arrived from the kitchen with small cups of traditional, very strong, Hungarian coffee and glasses of cool soda water.

'This is what I need,' I said, gulping the soda water and helping myself to more.

'It's so hot,' Paul said. 'What's the temperature?'

'About 38 degrees,' said Rézi. 'I just don't go out in the afternoons at all.'

The room, however, was shaded by the wooden blinds outside the windows, which cast a mellow light all around. 'Come and have a look from the balcony,' Miklós beckoned, picking up his lighter and putting another Marlboro to his lips as he headed for the adjoining room. Leaning over we could see, immediately below us, one of the girls we had noticed when we arrived. She was carefully counting a wad of 500 forint notes. 'Well, if you have any financial problems,' Miklós told Paul, 'just send Marion here,' and winked at me.

Chess players, mostly older men, sat on stone benches around stone tables, surrounded by small groups of silent onlookers, standing with hands clasped behind their backs. The gypsy children shrieked in the fenced ball-game area and, in the middle of the road, a cat played lazily with a rag attached to a piece of string.

It was too hot for me. I went back inside and chatted to Rézi about our travels through West and East Germany where, at the border, the officials had kept us for several hours and made us empty the car, before we could journey on to wonderful Weimar, and thence to Prague and Budapest. In East Germany we had been stopped five times by the police. There and in Czechoslovakia the oppressive atmosphere and the belligerence of officials had made us begin to wonder if we had made a serious error of judgement in coming to stay in Budapest. Paul and I had not mentioned our concern to each other, and it was dispelled completely as we crossed into Hungary, waved on by smiling border guards who did not even ask us to get out of the car.

The phone rang, and Rézi answered.

'That was Péter,' she told me, 'He'll meet you at the flat at five.'

I looked at the clock; just quarter past four. No hurry then, as the flat which we were to rent from Péter was quite near, just across the Danube on the Buda side. I helped myself to more soda water and idly turned the pages of the Hungarian newspaper lying beside me. I wondered if I would ever learn this language. A year before, at a party in England, we had met a Hungarian emigré who told us with some pride that it was a language impossible for a foreigner to learn. I wondered.

Miklós and Paul came back from the balcony and Rézi relayed the gist of Péter's call. Miklós picked up his small leather bag containing his identity card, monthly travel pass and wallet, and we left together, this time using the lift, which we had not noticed in the dark of our arrival. Rézi waved from the balcony as we squeezed into the car, me sitting on the top of the luggage on the back seat, Miklós nursing my guitar in front.

It was Saturday afternoon, so all the shops had closed at one o'clock, but the restaurants and *cukrászdák* (cake shops come cafés) were open and people emerged carrying parcels of cake. All along the boulevard people were strolling, slowly pushing pushchairs and licking ice-creams, looking into shop windows shaded by fading awnings. Others sat at tables under table parasols, chatting and drinking as crowded trams rumbled past, watched by people on the balconies above.

★★★★

We crossed the river from Pest to Buda and passed the many buildings of the University of Technology, then we turned into Vántus Károly Street. A quiet street of trees and small blocks of four-storey flats, with larger, ten-storey blocks not far away. 'You are on the third floor. There's a lift, and you've got a phone,' said Miklós. 'Two minutes to five.' Miklós looked at his watch with satisfaction. He prided himself on his punctuality and on his ability to estimate within a few minutes the journey time between any two places in the city. 'And here's Péter,' he added, seeing a bearded, portly figure approaching.

Péter, too, taught English, and was to spend the following year in London. His wife, Éva, had decided that she would spend the year with her parents in Dabas, some thirty miles outside Budapest. So their flat was free for us. We all shook hands, then Paul and I followed Péter and Miklós into the building and up to the third floor.

The flat was minuscule: one room, a kitchen, bathroom and narrow hall. Every possible space had been utilized – even the phone had to be housed in the meter-cupboard by the front door. Péter explained the workings of the washing machine, the cooker, the gas water-heater in the bathroom, and the sofa bed. He told us that, if anyone asked, we were to say that we were relatives of the man whose brass name-plate was on the door. In point of fact, Józsi bácsi had died some years before, but it was bureaucratically expedient for Péter and Éva to perpetuate his supposed existence. Moreover, Józsi bácsi, had he but known it, was at that moment up to his ears in organising a flat swap.

Most flats in the city were council owned and were rented out for a nominal sum. The flats varied from small ones of about 30 square yards in floor area, having one room and a kitchen but sharing a bathroom (often outside) with other tenants, to flats of up to 200 square yards. Originally, flats were allocated according to size of family, but in 1945 single tenants or small families occupying the larger flats had been forced either to move or have their flats partitioned. But by now, 1982, it was quite common to find one elderly person occupying a four room, 100 square metre flat, while next door a family with two or three children were living in one room with grandparents in the only other room. Since council flats could not be owned, they could not be sold, so there was much flat-swapping. Thus, a family like Péter and Éva and their young son wanting to move to a larger flat would advertise in the newspaper. Similarly, an elderly person in a flat so large that they could no longer cope with cleaning or heating it, would advertise for something smaller. And so a swap would be arranged. Pages of advertisements were to be found in the newspapers and it was such a swap that Péter and Éva were in the process of finalizing. So far the practice was entirely legal; however, the person offering the larger property always asked for a huge sum of money, possibly several hundred thousand forints (equivalent to four or five years' earnings) and this was totally illegal.

Péter and Miklós chatted for a while in Hungarian, leaving Paul and me to look around. From the window I could see a low, brick building with a playground surrounded by trees, presumably a school, and beyond was a ten-storey block of flats. Unhappily, I saw no record player or tape recorder; music was the core of our lives and it would be difficult to live without it until our things arrived from England.

'Where's the nearest shop?' I asked Péter.

'Well, there are a couple of small ones in the next street: a butcher, a greengrocer and grocer, but if you walk a bit further there's an enormous shopping centre called the Skála.

You can buy everything there from food to furniture. By the way, if you see any washing powder you should buy it. There's been a shortage, and though we've left you some, you'll soon need more.'

Whether it was the washing powder itself that was in short supply or the card used to make the boxes became the subject of a short debate, but whatever the reason, I made a mental note to buy some as soon as I found it.

The following day Miklós rang and invited us to lunch, and then we spent the afternoon in the flat, finding places for all our things. The building was in a quiet cul-de-sac, but after just one night we found there was a hub cap missing from one of the wheels of our car. Later we learned that since many spare parts were unobtainable, it was common practice for people to help themselves from other cars. In time, a wing mirror and a strip of silver trim also disappeared.

The following Monday we decided to try our hand at shopping. Miklós had loaned us some money to tide us over until we started earning, so with bags, dictionary and money in hand, we decided to try the Skála that Péter had mentioned. We walked past the building I took to be a school, down a quiet tree-lined street and into a busy main road. Opposite was the large modern building, just as Péter had described it.

We wandered along the aisles, surprised at the choice of goods in comparison with what had been available in the smaller shops we had visited during our earlier visits to Hungary. Cold meat and cheese were weighed at a counter, not pre-packaged, and I realised with alarm that as well as the language problem, we also had the metric system to grapple with. Of course I knew all about 1000 grams to the kilo, but how heavy, in ounces, was a 200 gram piece of cheese? Before I could calculate, it was my turn at the counter. I pointed to some cheese that looked slightly less oily than the rest and tried to show the size I wanted. So far so good, then we looked for milk. We could have found it with our eyes shut.

A sour smell hung around what were supposedly refrigerated cabinets. The milk, packed in plastic bags of half or one litre, floated in a pool that had leaked from bags which had burst. People were wiping their milk bags on a fetid cloth draped over the side of a crate, transferring the smell to their hands. A smudged line of purple ink was intended to indicate the sell-by date, but was hopelessly blurred.

Food items were at least easy to identify; cleaning things were not. Of the various bottles with pictures of kitchens on their labels, I found it impossible to decide whether they were for washing up or cleaning sinks or floors. Later, friends laughingly told me that there was probably no difference.

The dictionary was not much help because it would have taken too long to translate the lengthy instructions on the bottles. Opening one or two, we hazarded guesses according to smell and appearance as to what they were likely to contain. Unfortunately, washing powder was not in evidence anywhere.

We had decided to try to cook *pörkölt*, a rich casserole-type dish, since it seemed probable that ingredients for traditional Hungarian fare would be the easiest to come by. This entailed a visit to the butcher on our way home and Paul's using his few words of Hungarian; he had been on a summer course at the University of Debrecen the year before and had stayed with a Hungarian family who spoke no English. They had taught him to cook local dishes, so I left him to it. He had only to mutter the word *pörkölt* and the butcher made for one of the pig carcasses suspended from a hook on the wall. I looked around. A fly was crawling over a tray of chicken legs and others had settled on the salamis and sausages hanging above us. The meat was diced, thrown on a piece of white wrapping paper and slapped on the scales.

Our shopping over, we went home, where the first thing I did was wash the meat and pick off the bits of paper that had stuck to it. Next we had to find a container for the milk which remained in a leaking packet - and then to wash all the other things in the same bag, followed by the bag itself. (Afterwards bags of milk were always carried in a separate plastic carrier bag.)

It did not take many days to get used to pulling out the sofa every night to sleep on, after moving the armchair and coffee table; getting to grips with the rhapsodical gas water-heater in the bathroom which would alternately scald or freeze you depending on the gas pressure; and remembering that the phone, when it rang, was in the cupboard by the front door. Miklós had lent us a tape recorder and some cassettes and we had managed to find the BBC World Service on Péter's Russian radio; we had even seen Starsky and Hutch dubbed into Hungarian on the large black-and-white TV set that dominated the room.

There were no television broadcasts on Mondays. The official explanation was that on one day a week Hungarians should engage themselves in more meaningful activities, but our friends seemed to agree that it was a money-saving measure.

Cooking had become a chore, mainly because we could not find the ingredients to make the things we were used to eating at home in England, and we were becoming bored with *pörkölt*, and sliced pork fried in breadcrumbs, another everyday dish in Hungary. Also, as August gave way to September the price of tomatoes and other fruit and vegetables shot up, so most people turned to pickled gherkins and cabbage, on which we were not too keen.

The best piece of advice we were ever given about shopping was from Miklós: always to take at least a thousand forints, so that if we saw something we might need within the next six months, be it Sellotape or a tin of bacon, we could buy it because we could be sure we would not find it when we needed it. How invaluable that advice was, and how I rued not having followed it on those occasions when I did not have spare cash with me! However, Paul had found some washing powder, stacked high in the corner of a small tobacconist's.

We spent the first few weeks living from one day to the next, relying heavily for help and interpretation on Miklós and another friend, Bálint, whom we had met the previous summer. Listening to Bálint's English was rather like reading a literary masterpiece – his immense vocabulary and choice of phrase would put most English people to shame. His mother had been a famous translator from Russian and he himself was translating Hungarian poetry into English.

Paul's teaching at the Music Academy would only start at the end of September but he had to go there to discuss whom and what he would be teaching, and to obtain papers we needed for both residence and work permits.

Miklós had organised a group of young children for me to teach English to. They lived on a large housing estate and I was to teach them in a room in the attic of one of the blocks of flats. On the second occasion that I went there, one sunny, Monday afternoon, I found the children waiting for me outside as usual, but this time they were all standing around a spot on the path discussing something. One of the mothers approached me as I reached the children. 'A man jumped from the seventh floor and landed just here this morning as the children were going to school,' she explained. Miklós later informed me that not only was Hungary's suicide rate the highest in the world, but leaping out of high-rise flats the most popular method of maintaining the statistic.

Meanwhile, things were being arranged for me to teach for two weeks in Baja, a beautiful town on the Danube south of Budapest, which we had visited with Miklós two years previously.

Miklós and his closest friend János both taught English at the Karl Marx University of Economics in Budapest, but for some time it had been their ambition to start up their own school of English. Until January 1982, this had not been permitted, but now they were able to go ahead. In the meantime they had organised one or two English courses in factories or companies outside Budapest and were teaching there when they were not at the University. One such course was the one in Baja, designed for the manager and a small group of employees at 'Blévisz', a small furniture factory. The course was not held in the factory, but at a small 'holiday home' belonging to the company. This was on a tree-covered island in the Danube accessible only by a footbridge.

Most factories and companies in Hungary had these holiday homes, which varied from the extremely simple to the luxurious. Employees could stay there for a short holiday at nominal cost, and they were also used for company functions and visitors. Since Blévisz was a relatively small company, there were only four bedrooms, a shower room and an outside toilet, and the building was only used during the summer.

A few days before I was to start teaching I went to collect books and cassettes at the premises Miklós and János had leased for their school, Lingua. It was a ten-storey block, identical to those in the area where we lived, and right beside the river in Óbuda (Old Buda, now a suburb of Budapest). Óbuda has many old houses, courtyards with grapevines and flowers, wine-cellars and Roman ruins including a huge amphitheatre.

Miklós and János had leased two rooms on the sixth floor for teaching, with a small office, toilet, kitchen and storeroom. Heaps of books lay all over the floor of the larger classroom, along with newspapers, posters, a couple of tape-recorders and piles of cassettes. Someone was drilling holes for bookshelves and a blackboard, and in the corner was a pile of new chairs. In the corridor stood an old fridge, destined for the kitchen once it had been cleaned.

The drilling stopped for a moment. 'This is Pisti,' Miklós introduced me to their electrician friend, who smiled and asked a question in Hungarian. 'He wants to know why you've come to Hungary.'

'Tell him it's a long story,' I said as I climbed over a pile of books and an open bottle of some black alcohol which I failed to recognise even when I picked it up and smelt it.

16

'Here, try some,' said János, offering me his glass. 'It's medicinal.' It tasted like it; bitter and strong. This was Unicum – people either swore by it or hated it, and I quickly accepted a glass of wine instead.

Kneeling on the partly unrolled carpet, we searched for the books and cassettes I was to take to Baja. That done, János began to put some posters on the wall, and Miklós took his wallet from his leather bag and handed me a train ticket. 'I'll try to come and see you off at the station, but in case I can't make it, here's your ticket. Your train leaves from Déli station on Sunday at 1.40 pm. This is a first-class ticket; the factory pays, and Zsuzsa (one of the students) will meet you. I sent her a telegram today. I'll probably come down on Friday and see how it's going. The lessons are like last year, from 7 am till 3 pm with an hour for lunch. Make them work hard and fine them if they don't do their homework.'

Sunday arrived, still hot and sunny even now in September. Paul came to see me off and we found Miklós and János waiting for us on the platform of the beautiful new station. 'Just to make sure you've really gone,' said Miklós as I climbed on. The distance between platform and train is so enormous that old people usually throw their luggage up and then try to heave themselves in, often with the help of a good shove from a friend on the platform.

The train was not due to leave for another half-hour, but Hungarians always arrive early to settle themselves in with bags of bread, salami and beer. However, in the first-class compartments there were relatively few people in spite of the very small difference in cost. So we all got in to chat till I left.

Miklós gave me a pile of work he had marked for the group, then János wandered along the platform to buy something to drink. A stillness hung in the air on this hot Sunday afternoon, a quietness and laziness as we sat in the compartment drinking the cool juice János had found.

The guard blew his whistle. Paul kissed me, saying 'Good luck. I'll write,' and János pulled out a white handkerchief, brought specially for the occasion, and continued to wave it till the train was out of sight.

I was alone in the compartment, and though my intention had been to look through what I was to teach the next morning, I sat back lazily and watched the countryside roll past. Sunburnt fields, dusty tracks and higgledy-piggledy gardens full of flowers; mile upon mile of sunflower fields, their huge heavy heads turning to follow the sun, reflecting their Hungarian name '*napraforgó*', 'turning to the sun' flowers. The occasional horse and cart bumped along the unmade roads, and small groups of country people were picking paprika or hoeing the dusty ground. Their lunch baskets of beer and salami lay with their bicycles in the grass at the edge of the fields. The laden vines would soon be harvested and I saw many of the 'heron' water wells, their name an apt description of the long slender pole which stretched up, sharply defined against the blue sky.

Four hours later, as the shadows were beginning to lengthen, the train clanked across the enormous bridge over one of the widest stretches of the Danube, and into Baja. I dragged my things off the rack and leaned out of the window. Most country stations have only one platform, so along with everyone else I plodded across the rails to the station building. No Zsuzsa. I looked about, but without much hope, for Zsuzsa was a punctual, reliable person, and resigned myself to the long walk to Petöfi Island, some two miles from the station. She had obviously not received the telegram, and I cursed the Hungarian postal service as I carried my heavy bags through the town, passing through its lovely cobbled main square of imposing, early nineteenth century buildings, and on to the footbridge crossing over to the island.

The Blévisz holiday home was at the far end of the island, and I was dusty and exhausted by the time I arrived. In its garden a young couple sat drinking, and they looked at me questioningly as I staggered through the gate. I tried German: no luck. I pointed to myself and said, '*angol*,' meaning

English, then the name of the factory, its manager, and Zsuzsa, assuming that the couple must have some connection with Blévisz and might be able to help me.

The man stood up and took my bags into the kitchen. Nothing had changed since my last visit, particularly not the number of mosquitoes on the walls. Beckoning to me to follow, the man went back out, locked the door, spoke to the girl, and we all left the garden together.

Under the trees on a path by the water stood his car. We crossed the tributary of the Danube which separated Petöfi island from the town of Baja on a raft attached to a metal cable. This ferry was just large enough for one vehicle and after we had pulled ourselves across the water, we continued in the car to Zsuzsa's home.

My suspicions had been correct: the telegram had not arrived, and when I had failed to turn up by the earlier train Zsuzsa had assumed I was not coming. Neither she nor the Lingua premises had a phone, and in any case making a call to Budapest took hours and had to be booked in advance through the operator. I kissed Zsuzsa's parents in greeting, I had seen them the previous year when I had first taught in Baja, and again felt shock at the sight of her father's gnarled and twisted hands, completely crippled from his spell in a Russian camp. About seven hundred thousand Hungarians were rounded up at the end of the war as part of the reparations to Russia. They were told they were being taken for a few days to do '*malenkij robot*', a little job, but were used as forced labour for agricultural and other manual work. Those lucky enough to return did so only after two to four years, virtual skeletons. Zsuzsa's father had been one of the 'lucky' ones and survived, though he had since been totally unable to work; tens, maybe hundreds, of thousands had died in the severe conditions.

After a drink with the couple who had brought me, Zsuzsa took me out to her car and we set off to tell the others in the group that the course would start the following morning as planned.

The ochre and yellow plasterwork of the old one-storey houses were baking in the last mellow rays of the sun. Acacia trees, pruned to stand no higher than seven or eight feet lined the streets. Only the main road was tarmac, the others being mud in winter, dust in summer.

It was late by the time we got away from Jody's, the manager of Blévisz, an unashamed Anglomaniac who preferred the name Jody to his Hungarian name György, and had named his son Gordon. We sat in his garden eating watermelon, sandwiches and drinking wine till the mosquitoes became unbearable. 'I'll take you home,' said Jody.

'But you've been drinking,' Zsuzsa interrupted, a total drinkdrive ban being strictly enforced in Hungary.

'That's all right,' replied Jody with a wink.

We both knew what that meant. As one of the better-known personalities in the town he obviously had friends among the local police.

The days passed quickly, getting up at six, eating a quick breakfast of bread, cheese and tomatoes in the kitchen while Marika the caretaker, cleaned. During the first morning break one of the group would go off on his bike to the bridge and bring back a heap of '*lángos*', a deep fried batter-like bread sprinkled with salt, which we all ate hungrily with the coffee Marika had made. At the end of the afternoon we had a swim together in the river, and in the evenings we usually met in the town in a wine-cellar or sat outside at a café, or I went to Zsuzsa's. Once we saw a dubbed version of 'Carry on Cowboy', sitting on the wooden seats of the small cinema. The result was often that no-one had done their homework by the following morning, and as on past occasions, they paid a fine of five forints for each piece of work not done. Fines were also incurred for yawning, repeatedly making the same mistake, or arriving late. By the time Miklós arrived, we had collected quite a sum and he decided to buy a bottle of champagne and lay on a treasure hunt. This entailed the two of us in an amusing afternoon of pacing round the house, the garden, and the area down to the river, and an evening of writing instructions and clues. In the late afternoon Marika's husband turned up with a friend and caught a couple of carp in the river, and I shared in the wonderful fish soup for which Baja is justly famous. It bubbled red and orange in a huge, black cauldron over a fire in the garden while we all sat around in the amber glow, chatting and laughing.

To reach my room, I had to go up some outside stairs to a terrace from which four doors led into the bedrooms. Sometimes, in the afternoons, I sat on the terrace and looked over to the canoeists and the small ferryboat with its oarsman waiting to take passengers to the next island downstream, while on the far bank of the river sat a lone fisherman, and on the sand people sunbathed or read. Miklós had lent me a small battery-operated tape-recorder and a couple of cassettes of my favourite Hungarian music: *LGT* and *Zorán*, which I would listen to as I watched the canoeists.

On Monday morning we started work at seven as usual, but at ten o'clock Zsuzsa went with me to the police station to extend my thirty-day visa, leaving some work for the students. When we arrived at the office we found most of the wooden seats in the bare, stone-floored waiting room already occupied. No-one was talking, and although it was well past ten, the hatch doors in the wall opposite remained tightly closed. There was an atmosphere of silent resignation as the clock ticked on and still no-one came. 'Shouldn't we knock on the door or something?' I whispered to Zsuzsa when the clock showed almost eleven; she smiled and shook her head. There seemed to be no possibility of being dealt with before the specified closing time of noon, since most of the waiting people had arrived before us. We waited. Then finally at five minutes to noon, the hatch doors were opened and a woman said, 'We are now closing. Please come back tomorrow.' I looked round for some reaction from the other people, but they merely put their papers back in their pockets and ambled out into the sunshine. They were there again the following morning, as were we.

Two weeks passed quickly and then I was back in Budapest. Paul told me that in my absence Éva had called to explain that they had at last completed the flat swap, so that they, and therefore we, would be moving on the first of November. She had promised to take us to see the flat when I returned from Baja. The Music Academy had organised our residence permits for a year, so it would no longer be necessary to pay our monthly visit to the police station. The Academy had received word from the Hungarian removal company, Masped, that our container of goods had arrived from England, but we decided to delay delivery until we moved to the new flat.

October arrived, and with it, the autumn and the first cool mornings, a hint that the 'old women's summer' (Indian summer) was coming to an end. The children in the building opposite, not a school but a nursery, no longer had their midday nap on the balcony. When I had first seen the row of beds I thought it was a hospital. Children from the age of six months can be left in nurseries all day, leaving their mothers free to work. The majority of mothers leaving children under the age of three did so because the family could not have survived without the woman's earnings, not because she was eager to continue working.

Paul had started his first term teaching Musicology and English at the Liszt Academy, a splendid turn-of-the-century building which stands four storeys high on the corner of Franz Liszt Square and houses one of the city's main concert halls. As you enter and walk into an airy, vaulted foyer with a floor of red marble, you may hear a rehearsal of Verdi's *Requiem* by a visiting orchestra, or an internationally-famous musician practising before the evening concert. It is usually possible to go in to the hall and listen at the back. Past the snack bar and ticket office, any one of three staircases, again of red marble, will take you to the upper floors where the teaching and practice rooms are, rooms where Bartók, Kodály and a host of famous instrumentalists once taught.

By now I was at Lingua most days, teaching various groups of adults and children from the age of four. Things were slowly beginning to sort themselves out there, though with just four of us teaching, there were times when one of us had to cover another's lessons and this could result in long hours and heavy workloads. As well as Miklós, János and myself, there was Ancsa, who also taught at the Economics University. If she was busy and one of the others was in the country, I occasionally had days of teaching from 7.30 in the morning till 9 in the evening with only a few short breaks.

It was the policy of the school for everything to be 'English', with tea in the breaks instead of coffee, with milk of course, and there was a very informal, friendly atmosphere. After evening lessons, it became the custom for teachers and students to visit a nearby wine cellar, patronised by local working men, where we sat at heavy wooden tables in the semi-darkness under cart wheels transformed into 'chandeliers' drinking dry red wine and eating hunks of bread with raw onions. It was not unusual for the students to join in the singing which inevitably began as the evening wore on.

Something which had struck us even on our first visit to Hungary was that the espresso cafés and eating places, which seemed to constitute every third or fourth shop, were always full of people, even in the middle of the day. 'But how is it that they are not working?' I asked, a reasonable question in a country where unemployment was not only unknown, but illegal. The answer was always a shrug of the shoulders. The other fact we found difficult to understand was how people could afford to spend their days drinking and eating out when they earned relatively little. But it became clear when we started work: though the average monthly wage was only three or four thousand forints, the daily expenses of food, gas, electricity, and the rental of a state flat were incredibly low. A month's season ticket for unlimited travel on the very efficient public transport system with a choice of bus, trolley-bus, tram, or underground, was just 110 forints. The rent of an average two-room flat was some 200 forints a month, and food was heavily subsidised. Gas and electricity charges were nominal, while a cinema, theatre or even an opera house ticket could be had for ten forints. On the other hand, the price of a car, TV set or washing machine, not to mention a flat (about a million forints for a private one, half a million for a state flat) was totally out of reach for the majority. Thus, the whole ethic of saving money was alien; money was for spending.

To this had to be added one of the fundamental differences between working in Hungary and England: a Hungarian's salary is not his total income. Everyone had their 'second job'. For a teacher this might be giving private lessons, for a craftsman it meant extra private work at a higher rate of pay than his official job, either in flats or for one of the burgeoning small private firms. Official working hours were broadly from seven or eight in the morning till four or five in the afternoon. It is also true that many clocked in (or maybe did not) at their main job, then went out to do private work. This was particularly notorious in the building trade, where workmen would leave the site of a state block of flats to work on a private site, often 'redirecting' (as it came to be known) state building materials for the private job.

The succeeding days passed quickly in a whirl of teaching, shopping, and packing ready for the move. We had been to see the new flat on Dózsa György Street, a broad avenue with Heroes' Square and the City Park within a few minutes' walking distance. It lay on the Pest side of the river on the first floor of an old building and overlooked a large courtyard full of plants and flowers. There were two large rooms with twelve-foot high ceilings, a long kitchen, bathroom and toilet. But there were some disadvantages: there was no phone, and in our Buda flat we had got used to this luxury, and the flat was dark, a characteristic of courtyard flats. Even in the daytime it was necessary to have lights on. Nevertheless, we looked forward to moving somewhere larger and to having all our belongings delivered.

The move was completed quickly and easily. The large wall units were carried resting on a long belt wrapped around the shoulders of the two removal men. The elderly lady doing the swap with the Dózsa György flat was of course moving on the same morning, but by the time we arrived she and her belongings had already gone. Éva's aunt and uncle lived on the ground floor below us, and her uncle had taken it upon himself to look after the courtyard garden. He was proud to show us two certificates he had been awarded by the Budapest City Council in recognition of his work.

Our car had to stand in the road outside the main entrance to the building. This was the first time we had used it since arriving almost three months before, and we decided it was more of a problem than an asset, what with the parking difficulties and the steady disappearance of its bits and pieces. We decided to lend it to Miklós's brother, Dani, who lived in a small town outside Debrecen, since he would make good use of it and knew enough about cars to maintain it.

Éva supervised everything. Then as evening fell, she left us in candlelight – the electricity had gone wrong that very day. I watched from the uncurtained window as she waved and trotted down the worn marble steps into the courtyard, out of the huge wooden gate and into the dimly-lit street.

Snow and Settling
DÓZSA GYÖRGY STREET

On the day following our move our belongings were delivered. Despite the pages of advertisements from removal firms in the Yellow Pages in England claiming 'worldwide removal', or 'European removers' only one was in fact able to handle our things and then only as far as Vienna where a Hungarian company would have to collect them and take them on to Budapest. A typical response from the other 'worldwide removers' was, 'Hungary? What kind of politics they got there then?' followed by 'Sorry, we don't go to none of them communist countries.'

It had been difficult to decide what we might need and we had first thought of taking only clothes and some books and records. However, the removal firm told us that the quantity mattered not nearly so much as the distance, and since we had no idea what would be included in the rental of a flat in Budapest we eventually decided to take everything. We had no furniture since we were leaving a furnished flat (our piano and cat went to our friends Sue and Steve in Cambridge) but we took crockery, bedding, record-player, books, records almost everything we owned. The total weight of the container was some half a ton, so we were glad that the cost included delivery within Budapest to a ground or first-floor flat.

The lorry arrived late in the morning. Bálint was waiting with us to help with interpreting, should that be needed. The driver came up to our door, showed us the papers and indicated that we should follow him out into the street. The rear of the lorry stood open and inside was the huge wooden crate with our name chalked on it. We waited.

'He wants to know if you've got an axe to open the crate,' Bálint told us.

'No, we haven't,' Paul replied, 'and anyway, why hasn't he got one, and where are the other people to carry the things, or is he going to do it alone?'

Bálint translated. The driver took a packet of cigarettes from his shirt pocket, lit one, leant against the lorry and said, 'Well, I can't open the crate without an axe.' At that moment, Éva's aunt came through the gate on her way to the shop.

'Please ask her if she's got an axe,' I asked Bálint. She had, and she fetched it. The driver puffed out a final cloud of smoke, then swung himself up into the back of the lorry and began to open the container. One or two inquisitive people gathered round to watch. There were twenty-six large cardboard boxes inside.

The driver beckoned to Bálint, 'Help me get them down onto the pavement, will you?' he asked. The fact that delivery had been prepaid did not concern him. If we did not help it seemed he would be quite happy just to stand and smoke.

Gradually we unloaded them all. 'Now what?' Paul asked Bálint, 'Don't tell me we've got to carry them all the way up to the flat?' We did. It began to rain as we started the long trek from the street, through the gate across the courtyard and up the steps. We were all sweating, cold and damp by the time we had finished. The driver held out a paper to be signed.

'He says you have to pay 400 forints for delivery,' Bálint told us.

'What? We paid in England,' we replied.

The man shrugged his shoulders. 'They always say that, these foreign removal companies,' he said. It seemed pointless to try to prove our point by showing him the English language contract, so we decided to pay him and sort it out later at the Masped office.

'You have to give a tip,' said Bálint, a Hungarian mania which the Hungarians themselves cannot explain, especially since service is grudging at best and non-existent at worst. We gave him 500 forints which he pocketed disdainfully, and muttered complainingly as he went back to his van.

Bálint had to leave us then, so Paul and I began to push the boxes through the main room and into the second room which we had decided to use only as a store for the time being, both for our own things and some of Eva's that we didn't need. There was a ring at the door. A man and a woman, both in green uniform, informed us that they were from the customs and that we must not unpack any of the boxes until they had checked everything. Luckily, one of them spoke a little German. We led them into the back room. 'Now, we need to see your record player, tape recorder and amplifier,' they said. We had no idea which box they might be in, the boxes were labelled, 'Wardrobe', 'Books and sundries', 'Kitchen' and 'Miscellaneous'. The choice seemed to be between 'Sundries'' or 'Miscellaneous'. The man and woman settled themselves on top of a heap of plastic bags full of Eva's bedding and laundry and waited for us to find the things.

Slowly and unenthusiastically we started to open boxes and rummage through them. It did not take too long to find the amplifier and tape recorder, but the record player was elusive. Having been through twenty-four boxes, all that was left were the two large wardrobe boxes: carefully packed among our clothes lay the record player. The man and woman meticulously noted down the serial numbers and then asked, 'Have you got anything like a computer, television or other tape recorder?'

'Nothing,' we replied, 'only that small radio over there, an old sewing machine and a typewriter.'

'You understand that you are not allowed to sell any of these things and that when you leave the country we will check that you still have them?'

'We'll also need a list of all your other things,' the man said, indicating our heaps of boxes and belongings.

'You mean we have to list every book?' asked Paul, his voice touched with hysteria. 'We've got about 600 books and the same number of records.'

'And you want me to write down every pair of socks and shoes?' I asked incredulously.

The customs officer considered. 'Well, if you write down something like fifty history books, one hundred music books.. you know.. you needn't write down all the titles.'

'And the clothes?' I asked.

'Oh, just write down.. have you got a fur coat?'

I shook my head. He sighed. He obviously considered the whole situation as ridiculous as we did. Resuming his seat on top of the bags he said, 'You're from England, aren't you?' We nodded. 'Musicians?'

'I'm teaching at the Music Academy,' Paul replied.

'My son's a violinist. He's in an orchestra in West Germany,' he told us proudly. 'It's very difficult for musicians here. It's a small country and there aren't many orchestras. Anyway, the pay's so bad they have to spend all their time teaching. They have no time to practise, and no-one wants more than one rehearsal because they lose their teaching time and money. Then people wonder why the standards aren't what they should be.'

This was a situation we too were learning about – the standard of orchestras we had heard bore no resemblance to that of the playing of the students in the Academy, many of whom went abroad to work at the first opportunity. The customs man chatted a little longer, the woman saying nothing, and then having put his hat back on and the sheaf of papers back in his case, they left.

We felt very much at home in this new flat, though it was far from ideal from many points of view. Perhaps the worst fault was that we always had to have the lights on except on the very brightest days. The kitchen had no proper sink and no hot water, what it did have was something made of cast iron, painted white, comparable in appearance only to a urinal. This was attached to the wall with a single cold tap above, and it had many small holes like a colander, and no plug. We used it for peeling potatoes or vegetables, but washing-up could only be done by bringing a bowl of hot water from the bathroom, and standing it on the table. Gradually we unpacked our boxes and found to our amazement that not a single item had been broken.

It was November; dark, cold and cheerless. The few foreign tourists disappeared, and the Hungarian winter 'uniform' of black leather jackets and coats was once again apparent. Street and shop lighting was dim, and we were glad of our warm flat. All Hungarian homes, even down to the simplest peasant houses, have two sets of windows, an extremely effective form of double glazing, and are generally heated to a level uncomfortable for anyone wearing more than a T-shirt.

In the week following our move we went to the embassy to register our change of address, as was recommended for all foreign residents. The embassy also housed the British Council library, which contained a good number of both books and records, as well as a selection of daily papers and magazines. Most Hungarians, for whom the library actually exists, were afraid to go into the building. To do so had once been illegal, and even now they feared being reported by the policeman on the door. Foreign newspapers were only otherwise available in the large hotels, but even then our friends preferred to ask us to buy a paper or a magazine for them rather than go into the hotel themselves.

On some days I still began teaching at 7.30 am, which meant I had to leave home at 6.30. I was amazed that even so early in the morning, I had to wait for the third tube at Keleti station before I could push my way on.

Keleti railway station is an imposing structure, its entrance facade flanked by large statues with James Watt on one side and on the other, Robert Stephenson. The station is situated in a run-down area with a proliferation of illegal street traders who sold quartz watches and calculators. The station itself was always alive with a colourful assortment of widely contrasting people – the Vienna Waltzer bringing the ostentatiously well-dressed Viennese, the trains from Romania with Transylvanian-Hungarians shouldering heavy bundles of indeterminable content and baskets of food, drink and the occasional live chicken or goose. The trains to and from Moscow were always overcrowded with Russian soldiers, with their huge flat-topped hats which looked as though they had a long-playing record in them. Keleti was one of the meeting points for Hungarian conscripts, self-conscious in their new uniforms and short haircuts, their parents nearby with carrier bags full of their sons' possessions. Small stalls crowded the entrance and platforms selling newspapers and refreshments surprisingly including fresh chestnut purée and cream in small plastic cups.

Outside the station was a large stairway leading down to the underground and to a pedestrian area with stone seats and one or two espresso bars. There are three underground lines in Budapest, the first was built not long after the first London one, with trains rather like underground trams. The other two lines, built on the Russian model, are very deep under the ground, and the trains are spotlessly clean, spacious and fast.

Following my walk from home to the station and the tube journey (which takes you under the Danube) I took the *Hév*, a green, electric train which travels out to the suburbs. This goes directly to Óbuda and the Lingua School, and then on to Szentendre – a picturesque Serbian town on the Danube, home of artists, art galleries, and tourists.

As November wore on, our thoughts turned to our projected trip to West Germany to visit my aunt and her family. My mother and brother were to travel from England so that we would all meet at my aunt's for Christmas. By far the cheapest way for us to travel was by train through Czechoslovakia and East Germany, though this would entail obtaining visas. Miklós advised us to book our seat-reservations early, so along the three of us went to the central travel office. On the ground floor were long queues waiting for hard currency – available only every three years, since Hungarians could obtain a passport only once every three years. If they wanted to travel abroad more often they needed a letter of invitation from a friend or relative which guaranteed that the friend would meet all their expenses while they were in the foreign country.

31

On the first floor was the crowded *büfé* – a kind of snack bar where you could get anything from coffee and cake to alcohol and cigarettes, and on the second floor was the ticket office.

'Just leave it to me,' said Miklós.

We stood next to the glass window and waited until its beige curtains were whisked aside to reveal a seated woman, cigarette in hand, and then waited while she concluded a chat with a colleague.

'Yes?' she eventually asked.

'We would like two tickets for the train to East Berlin on December 20th,' Miklós said.

'Before you can buy a ticket you have to have a seat reservation.'

'Where can I get that?' asked Miklós.

'There,' she said, pointing to the glass window immediately next door to her own.

'Thank you.'

We moved over to the new window. After a few minutes the curtains opened to reveal the same woman. 'Yes?'

'Two seat reservations for the train to East Berlin for December 20th,' Miklós repeated.

'First or second class?'

'First, no-smoking.'

'That will be 24 forints.'

Miklós paid and she closed the curtains. We walked back to the first window. 'Can I see your passport?' she asked as Miklós handed over the seat reservations. Miklós grimaced and gestured to me to show my passport. 'You can't pay in forints if you're travelling on a Western passport.'

'But this lady works here and earns here – look, here's her residence permit,' Miklós replied.

'Well, then you need a special permit from the National Bank.'

'Thank you,' said Miklós, taking my sleeve and pulling me away. 'Don't worry, I'll try at Keleti station.'

The following day he went back alone, where a young, less-experienced girl happily sold him the tickets. The total cost, with a first-class sleeping compartment return to Berlin was 3,000 forints (about 40 pounds).

The following week I went to get our Czech visas. I found myself in a large, smoky room with many Arabs all filling in visa application forms. The room was sparsely furnished with wooden chairs and tables. Yellowing posters of Czechoslovakia – whether from age or cigarette smoke I could not decide – graced the dingy wallpaper, and on the long wall opposite were two kitchen-like hatches, both closed. I went to one where two people were already standing. After a few minutes the doors opened but when my turn came I found that the woman spoke neither English nor German, only Czech and Hungarian. This was not a great deal of help, nor very logical, since neither Hungarians nor Czechs needed visas. I sat down to fill in the forms. Four identical forms had to be completed for each person, carbon paper was not available and anyway a poster on the wall stated that carbon copies would not be accepted. In addition, only the first form had any other language apart from Czech on it, so in filling in the subsequent forms it was necessary to keep referring back to the first. Two photographs were needed for each person and as I had only one, I decided to leave the crowded, smoke-filled room and return another day.

I took the trolley-bus home. The red trolley-buses had been a gift, though many considered it a dubious one, from the Soviet Union to Hungary. The numbering on the trolleys begins at 70, Stalin's age when the gesture was made. They seemed to be fitted only with a brake and accelerator, which might account for their erratic variations of speed, causing elderly women laden with shopping to lurch backwards at great velocity from one end of the bus to the other, taking other startled passengers with them every time the traffic lights changed to green. The small interior was often stifling and smelly – in summer from sweaty, sticky armpits, in winter from mothballs and unwashed clothes. While the underground covered large distances quickly and the trams and buses shared the main road, the trolley-bus (or the geriatric express as we dubbed it) alternately crawled and lurched along narrow backstreets.

I managed to push my way to the door one stop before my usual one, having decided to pop into the small corner self service shop on my way home. In order to keep the heat in the shop, a thick, green felt curtain had been hung inside the door. I fought my way through its heavy folds only to find there were no baskets. This necessitated two further forays through the curtain, first to the door to get a basket and then back, at the same time trying to avoid being knocked out by new customers coming through the doors.

Bread stood on a metal trolley, with a small piece of paper bearing the day of baking stuck into the dough of each one. It was 'today's' but when I prodded it I realised it was already hard enough to have reached the category of an offensive weapon. Behind me, other fingers squeezed and prodded too. Nearby lay a pile of tissue paper, barely large enough to cover half a loaf, for the purpose of wrapping the bread – a purely symbolic gesture to hygiene considering its handling by customers, the delivery man, shop staff and not forgetting the smears of sour milk in the plastic shopping baskets.

I joined the queue at the checkout. There was an argument going on regarding some bottles which a man insisted he had bought there, but which the cashier was equally determined not to accept. (Nearly all glass jars and bottles have a deposit.) 'This isn't one of ours, is it?' called the woman to a girl behind the cheese counter.

She shrugged, 'How should I know?'

'Try the shop down the road,' the cashier concluded, putting the empty bottles with the man's shopping and starting to deal with the next customer's basket. The man continued to argue but was studiously ignored.

Finally came the turn of the middle-aged woman in front of me. She wore the characteristic black leather coat, but set

34

off against this was a pair of white training shoes with fluorescent green laces. She put her basket on the shelf next to the till, and the cashier began to ring up the prices, transferring the items to an empty basket. Then, quite without warning, as she put her hand on a litre bag of milk, it burst, squirting over both herself and everyone and everything within a radius of a foot or two. She sighed and called, 'Ágnes, bring the bucket, will you?' whereupon a girl appeared from behind another curtain, bucket and cloth in hand. The queue waited while the cashier slowly and deliberately wiped her blue nylon overall, the till, the shelf and the floor, before handing the milk-soaked cloth to the customer to wipe her purchases in the basket.

Having fought my way back out through the green curtain, I headed for home. The black cobbles of Dózsa György Street shone as the subdued light of the lamps was reflected from the first, melting flakes of snow. As I walked into the entrance I had a quick look in our letterbox, one of many, rusty, metal boxes whose keys did not fit, took out a letter and a folded piece of paper and made my way across the courtyard and up the steps.

Once inside the flat I saw that the letter was from *Masped*. I did not open it as I would not be able to read it. The other was a note from Éva saying she would call to see us at the weekend. Of course, the rent. I walked over to the wardrobe and felt under a pile of sweaters where we kept the envelope containing our money. Current accounts with a cheque-book were something unheard of, and practically all transactions, from buying a car to buying a flat were conducted in cash. On one of our summer visits Paul had gone by train with János to a small town in the country to buy a hi-fi. János took some 30,000 forints in a paper bag which he clutched to himself throughout the journey. Our pay went into the envelope in the wardrobe and if it did not stretch till the 2nd of the following month, state pay-day, we borrowed from friends. This was common practice and not at all something to cause embarrassment, but on this occasion, it was alright, we had enough.

Paul arrived home a little after me, snow melting on his coat. I briefly described my trip to the Czech embassy and handed him the letter from *Masped*. 'They want another 200 forints from us,' Paul said.

'What! What for?'

'I don't know, can't understand that bit.'

'Well, they're not getting anything,' I retorted. 'First we pay in England, then we have to carry our own boxes and also pay for the privilege? And now they want more? They ought to be paying us!'

Paul threw the letter in the bin.

We started to cook a simple dish, *paprikáskrumpli* (potatoes in paprika) which we had been taught to make by the secretary who worked in the Liszt Society office in the Music Academy. She had invited us to supper and we had cooked it together. A Hungarian meal without paprika powder is practically inconceivable. Even the scrambled egg breakfast I had eaten on the train had been cooked with it and every cruet set has salt, pepper and paprika. In England it is a rather innocuous powder but in Hungary there are many varieties, from the sweet *csemege* to the lethally hot *erős*. But the main surprise for us was that paprika is a vegetable. The September fields are bright yellow and red with it. It is often compared to the more familiar red and green peppers, but actually bears little resemblance to them. The yellow, sweet paprika is richer in Vitamin C than an orange, and won a Nobel prize for the man who discovered this. It is commonly eaten raw for summer breakfasts with huge, sweet tomatoes and bread. The hot, red variety is hung in weighty clusters to dry and ripen around the doorways and windows of peasant houses, especially in the town of Kalocsa. This one does resemble the chili. Another hot variety is the cherry paprika, round and red. Paul had once made the mistake of supposing it to be a small tomato in his soup, had eaten it whole and practically exploded on the spot.

Another useful source of recipes was Paul's students. He had asked one of his English groups to write out their recipes for a favourite dish. One boy in the group, a violinist called Tamás, began with an introduction explaining that as one of eight children, and the son of a busy doctor, he would often cook at home. He gave us his recipe for *gulyás* (goulash). For practically all visitors to Hungary it comes as somewhat of a surprise to find that *gulyás* is a soup. It is actually named after the *gulyás* (cowherds) who cooked their meals in an iron pot over an open fire on the great plains in the East of Hungary. The thick stew-like meat dish we associate with the word 'goulash' is what is cooked in Austria and Germany. Hungarian *gulyásleves* is a hot and spicy soup cooked with beef and potatoes and paprika and usually eaten with hunks of fresh bread. Paul and Tamás would often discuss cooking before the lesson started, causing one of the numerous women who sit along the corridors of every floor of the Academy (rather like attendants in a museum, though here no-one seems to be quite sure what their function is) to shoo them away complaining of hunger.

As we finished eating I felt a twinge in a tooth. I knew it was bound to happen sooner or later because I had had an abscess drained and a temporary filling in July before we had left England. 'What shall I do?' I asked Paul.

'Why don't we ask the neighbours? There's bound to be a dentist around here.'

The following morning we knocked on the neighbours' door. They were very quiet people and up to now we had only passed the time of day on the stairs, but we had been told by Éva that the woman spoke English and German. There was no-one at home.

Snow covered the plants in the courtyard and lay in dirty, melting pools on the old mats in the entrance to the building. Outside it had been shovelled to the side of the pavement and formed a white wall between pedestrians and the traffic. The caretaker of every building is responsible for sweeping the pavement in front of it, while veritable armies of the most downtrodden looking men and women can be seen at midnight in minus twenty degrees, chipping away with their spades at the ice on paths and roads.

The snow brightened the gray and black facades of the smog-coated buildings. The pollution in Budapest often reaches intolerable levels, with two-stroke cars and buses belching out clouds of black smoke. Clothes, hair, curtains, everything becomes filthy in no time, the once-beautiful stonework blotted out by grime. Many Hungarians I met had the image of London, not to say of England, as being permanently shrouded in a smoggy haze and were frankly sceptical and offended when I suggested that Budapest was far more polluted than any city I had yet visited. We noticed it particularly when we returned from the countryside. It was often suffocating.

I had intended taking the trolley-bus to the Czechoslovakian embassy again, but changed my mind when I saw that one had broken down on the corner. The driver had got out and was trying to pull down the two long arms attached to the electric wires above. One came down without difficulty, the other would not, which meant that the next trolley to come along would be unable to get past.

Instead, I took a tram and soon found myself once again in front of the two hatches in the wall of the visa department. This time both were closed with a few people waiting at each. I waited too. Then, as one of the pairs of doors opened, those at the hatch at the far end of the room ran to join the other queue. I stood at the end and waited for my turn. The woman dealt with four or five people and then shut the doors. Those of us who remained waited again, when suddenly the far doors opened, sending us scuttling back to the other hatch. After one more such stampede, I was able to hand in my papers and flee the building.

I had an evening lesson at Lingua with a favourite group of students. They were all studying at the Foreign Trade College but also had jobs, mainly with foreign trade companies. They were a very humorous, enthusiastic and interesting group –

one of them, Anthony, had not long retired from the Hungarian national ice-hockey team and his hobby was poetry. Following our lesson, including the customary tea break, we piled into the cars of whoever had one and headed back into town. We had decided at the end of the lesson that the following week we would have a party.

I called in on Miklós on my way home. Sitting at the table was Endre, who was interested in working at Lingua. Endre stood up as I walked towards him. 'Hi, I'm Endre – Andrew,' he said. His pronunciation was impeccable, quite the best I had yet heard from any Hungarian. He was strong, heavily built, and talked at break-neck speed in both Hungarian and English.

'Where did you learn English?' I asked.

'In Warsaw,' he replied, 'Polish is my first foreign language, though.'

I could say nothing. He began to gather up his newspapers, the Herald Tribune and Time magazine from the table, swallowed the last mouthful of cognac and pulled on his fur hat. 'I hope we'll meet again,' he said to me, 'Miklós tells me you're living on Dózsa György Street. That's not far from us; I'll drop in some time,' and flashing me a huge grin he slapped Miklós on the back and walked out of the door.

'What do you think, should we employ him?' Miklós asked me.

'Well, I don't know what kind of a teacher he is, but his English is incredible.'

Miklós considered. 'He's in a mess. He and his wife Kati decided to leave Hungary this summer, and overstayed their 30-day visa in West Germany by a month. Kati wrote a letter to the headmaster of the school where she was teaching Russian, telling him all her negative feelings about Hungary, and later decided that she wanted to come back after all. Now, of course, their passports have been impounded and they're in trouble with the police.'

I arrived home to find Paul cooking and with the news that he had spoken to our neighbour about my toothache. 'He's a surgeon at a hospital in a place called Baross Road,' Paul told me. 'He said that if we go there tomorrow morning at nine o'clock he'll meet us and take us to the dentistry department.'

'I'll have to ring Miklós about my 7.30 am lesson and see if he or János can do it,' I said, pulling my boots back on and checking that I had some two-forint coins.

I stomped over the snow to the two telephone boxes on the corner. I picked up the receiver in the first one; it was totally dead. The second one gave me a line, but try as I might, I could not get the money into the slot. Banging the door behind me, I walked down the road to Keleti station. The only other phonebox en route to the station allowed me to dial and insert my money, but when the receiver was picked up at the other end, my money was swallowed and I was left with the dialling tone, my money gone. Swearing softly, I made for the 24-hour post office in the station courtyard. Shouting emanated from a couple of the phone boxes inside the entrance of the Post Office, their occupants struggling to overcome the technical deficiencies of the instruments. It no longer puzzled me that most things were organised by going personally to see people – it was quite literally quicker and considerably less wearing on the nerves than trying to make a phone call.

Three boxes stood vacant – not surprisingly. Two were totally dead whilst in the third although you could hear the voice of whoever you were phoning they were oblivious of even your most frantic shouts. I stood outside one of the occupied booths and waited. I looked at my watch, half an hour since I had left home. I could have gone to Rákóczi Square in that time. I shivered. Eventually I got through. Miklós agreed to take my lesson, and when I put the receiver back, my two forints dropped back down to me. Just like a fruit machine: you lose some, you win some, but generally you lose.

A group of snow-workers dressed in fluorescent, orange jackets were smoking to keep warm, their spades leaning against a closed flower booth. Their warm breath formed clouds which hung in the stinging cold of the night air. I stamped up the road to get some feeling back into my numbed feet, wondering what these poor people could possibly earn and what desperate circumstances had necessitated their having to undertake such work.

The following morning we looked up a few words concerning teeth and dentistry in the dictionary and went to the hospital. It was a large, red brick building, and at a few minutes past nine our neighbour came down the staircase. He shook hands and walked off down a corridor, beckoning to us to follow.

There was a long queue of people standing the length of the corridor, looking utterly bored. It was only as we were ushered into a room at the far end that I realised they were all waiting to see this same dentist. Our doctor neighbour said a few words to the dentist, whereupon I was directed to the dentist's chair and Paul took a seat by the window. I saw with relief that the equipment was modern and new, and in fact exactly the same make as my English dentist had. It took only a painless moment to lance the gum and prescribe me some antibiotics. He said the tooth would probably have to come out sooner or later but it could wait. Thanking him, Paul tried to press some money into his hand, we had been told this was expected for private treatment, but he categorically refused and smilingly opened the door back into the corridor. Sheepishly we walked past the row of people but observed not the slightest reaction, this kind of queue-jumping by friends of staff was obviously not uncommon.

November 7th, the anniversary of the Russian revolution, was a national holiday, but an uneventful one. When I asked my students how it was celebrated, they merely replied that more people than usual got drunk that day. Nevertheless, it was remarkable to us how the authorities changed the days of the week to give several free days in succession. November

7th fell on a Thursday, which would have been a national holiday. However, it was decided to make Friday a day off work, making a three-day weekend. Saturday's half-day would be worked on Thursday instead. Such changes were usually announced through the media and were generally adhered to. However, it did happen that individual companies decided to vary these changes causing particular confusion for self-employed people who could find themselves expected to be in two places on the same day.

By the end of November we had all the necessary visas and tickets to travel to West Germany for Christmas and a reserved sleeper on the train. The East German embassy, though forbidding and unfriendly, was quick and efficient, and the visas cost a fraction of the Czechoslovak ones.

The time leading up to our departure was filled with looking for Christmas presents, perusing the countless covered stalls that had sprung up to line the streets and fill the squares, selling everything from candles and jewelry to Matchbox cars and tubes of Smarties, along with gaudy Christmas decorations. In one of the subways I passed a cluster of bystanders watching a game which is played here and there around the city. Three upturned matchboxes are placed on a cardboard box, one with a small red marble beneath it. The boxes are then slid about at lightning speed while the gamester calls, 'Now you see it, now you don't,' occasionally lifting one of the matchboxes to reveal the red marble beneath. At double or quits you could bet five hundred forints on the box you thought concealed the marble when they finally came to rest. Obviously, some sleight of hand guaranteed you never chose the right one. I walked on, thinking how very many aspects of Hungarian life in general were epitomised in this game: an exciting swirl of activity, nothing where you thought it was, and a feeling of bewilderment at the end of it all.

I had written some thirty Christmas cards to friends and relatives in England, and hoping to find shorter queues in the evening decided to call in at Nyugati (western) station's twenty-four hour post office one evening after a class at Lingua. There was a young friendly-looking man behind one of the counters, so I stood myself behind the two or three others in the queue. When my turn arrived I pushed the heap of cards towards him under the glass. He stared at me in disbelief.

'Air mail, please,' I said hopefully.

'All of them?' he enquired. I nodded. 'This will take a long time,' he said, and then looking over the top of the glass he shouted to the other end of the large room, 'Bring this lady a chair, will you?' I turned to look in the direction he had shouted and saw a door open at the far end of the post office. A middle-aged man emerged carrying a wooden chair and approached me. Without gesture or comment he placed the chair next to me and then ambled off. I wondered if this was supposed to be a joke, but no-one was smiling. I sat down. It was not a joke: it took thirty-five minutes to weigh and stick the appropriate stamps and airmail stickers on my cards.

Together with Miklós, Rézi, János and his wife Márta, we had a pre-Christmas gathering and giving of presents, lighting the candles on the tree and eating the traditional bejgli, a kind of pastry swiss-roll filled with poppyseed or ground walnuts.

★ ★ ★ ★ ★

Our train, the Meridian Express, was due to leave Keleti station at 2.30 pm. We lugged our cases down to the street corner and on to the tram. Miklós, János and his brother Gyuri met us on the platform brandishing the customary white handkerchiefs.

'Now, got everything?' asked Miklós.

'Tickets, passports, visas, money?' János continued.

We smiled, and Paul slipped off one of his boots. 'Have a look,' he said, stretching the top of his socks to reveal a second one underneath, and just discernible near the heel, some pound notes between two layers.

'You needn't have bothered, they won't search you,' laughed Gyuri. As 'Hungarians' we were not permitted to have more than a minimal amount of western currency, yet we would have to pay for our ticket from East Berlin to Braunschweig in West German marks. The guard began slamming doors shut so we climbed aboard and hung out of the window waving until the three white handkerchiefs had merged with the falling snow.

By four o'clock it was dark. We were due at East Berlin's Ostbahnhof at 8 am the following morning. To break up the evening we decided to eat in the restaurant car, and began the long trek down the train past compartments of Hungarians chatting over beer and salami, and smokers lining the corridors and looking out at the red lights of level crossings as we rattled past. I was walking behind Paul, and something caught my eye where his boots and trouser legs met. A five pound note had worked its way out between the two pairs of socks and was about to fall to the floor. I pulled it out, but another note emerged with it, so we ducked into the next empty compartment and removed all the money to my handbag, hoping that Gyuri was right.

The food was simple and tasty; the dimly-lit restaurant car all but deserted with the two waiters and the chef playing cards and drinking at one of the empty tables. The ticket inspector came in as we were paying, checked our tickets and then joined the waiters and chef.

By 11 pm we were fast asleep, having crossed the Hungarian-Czech border. This was a lengthy process, with checks on passports and visas first by the Hungarians and then by the Czechs who also insisted we fill in a form declaring our possession of a camera – to prevent us from selling it on the train.

At 5 am we reached the Czech-East German border. Lights snapped on in our compartment and voices barked, 'Aufstehen, aufstehen!' ('Get up, get up!). I sat up. The border guard pointed to the suitcase opposite me, saying 'Aufmachen!'

('Open it!'). I did so, and after a short search he turned on his heel and left. He was followed by another guard to check the passports and visas, a farcical few minutes of scrutinising our photos, then us, then the photos again. Finally they left and we sank back into sleep.

At six we awoke to a view of grey, snow-covered houses as we slowly approached East Berlin. Our train to Braunschweig was due to leave at 10.30 am from Friedrich-strasse and we still had to get tickets and cross the border. We arrived punctually at 8 am, bought two tickets for the overground city train and made for Friedrichstrasse, the cross-over point to the west. Passing an open kiosk we bought some coffee which turned out to be undrinkable. The S-bahn was exactly the same as the green Budapest *Hév* and just as busy, but its atmosphere was completely different. It was all so quiet and gray, so very subdued, hardly anyone seemed to be talking.

When we arrived at Friedrichstrasse we looked for some sign to tell us the way to the border crossing. Nothing. We followed everyone else down the steps into a concrete area with ticket offices and I asked a man for directions. 'Over there,' he said, pointing out into the street. We bought our tickets to Braunschweig and carried our suitcases outside. We looked around and caught sight of the end of a queue of people behind some bushes on the opposite side of the road and went to join them. The long queue stretched into a prefabricated building and the first thing we noticed was the age of the people. They were all elderly. Some looked at us curiously, realising we must be foreigners since no-one under retirement age in East Germany could obtain an exit visa.

The queue shuffled slowly forwards and as we reached the front we saw the guards checking passports – two checks and then inside for the baggage search. The atmosphere was tense, no-one talked and yet the officials spoke always with raised voices. The final check took place in what reminded me of the starting boxes used in horse races: narrow, metal aisles with a closed door at the end. I walked in, noticing that above and around me were mirrors and glaring flourescent lighting. After several long looks alternately at my face and my photo, I heard a buzzer and the door opened just long enough for me to carry my case through. On the other side stood more guards, who watched as I stood and waited for Paul to follow me.

Finally, we walked up the steps to the platform with still half an hour in hand. The kiosk selling tea and coffee was closed, so we sat on a bench in the cold draughts coming from broken panes of glass in the station roof. As I looked up I saw with disbelief that in the girders above us, guards were walking, looking down at us, guns in hand, followed by alsatian dogs. There was also a small, glass look-out box under the roof in which sat another guard. My attention was then diverted by a voice shouting over the loudspeaker for someone to remove his suitcase from the white line painted along the platform. Three or four armed guards stood at intervals along this line, one with a dog.

A small group of old people had gathered near our bench, nervously checking their watches against the station clock and each asking the other, 'Have you got your seat reservation?' at which the other showed their ticket.

'Have you got a seat reservation?' one old lady said, looking at me.

'No,' I replied, and before I could proffer an explanation she interrupted me.

'Well, you can't travel on this train without a seat reservation,' at which one or two of the others murmured agreement.

'We've come from Budapest,' I said, 'you can't get reservations for this train there.'

She shook her head, 'They won't let you travel without one,' she repeated.

The train rumbled in. Before it came to a standstill a voice rasped over the loudspeaker, 'Nicht einsteigen! Nicht einsteigen!' ('Do not get in!'). We waited. Two of the guards

46

who had been standing along the white line moved to opposite ends of the train and began to search each compartment, while a third jumped down onto the rails alongside the train. He walked along its entire length while the alsatian walked underneath in search of potential escapees hanging under the train. Finally, the inspection completed, they waved up to the guards in the girders above.

People stood silently watching from the opposite platform, which had previously been obscured by the S-bahn train. It was then that I realised that we were not in a different station. Our border-crossing had been no more than changing platforms at Friedrichstrasse. The guards above were to stop the people opposite from crossing to our train.

The voice sounded again. 'Einsteigen!' ('Get in!'), which sent the elderly pensioners scuttling for the doors. We followed, only to find that they all had seat reservations in one carriage, the rest of the train being quite empty. Having settled ourselves in an empty compartment we watched as we moved slowly out of the station and across East Berlin towards the infamous wall. The railway passed right over it, and though I had seen stretches of the border in West Germany, this was chilling: barbed wire fences, a minefield, watchtowers, guards with dogs, and the grey wall bisecting a street, with a blackened church standing deserted next to it. It was unimaginable that anyone could escape by this route.

Then West Berlin: bright Christmas lights, fur coats, shiny cars, noise, colour, confident young people laughing with Walkmans and new shoes, sprawling on to the train. Through West Berlin and back into East Germany where, in the villages, high concrete walls separated the tracks from the street, and on the railway side of the wall, six-inch spikes were implanted in the ground for those trying to make it over the top. At the final border at Marienborn, we could see guards training alsatian dogs to pursue escapees.

Christmas came and went, the traditional mixture of too much food and too little exercise. It was a pleasure to go shopping where you were sure of finding what you wanted, only the choice was intimidating. And yet, we felt keen to return to Budapest when the time came. Endre had rung to ask me if I could find a doctor willing to issue a medical certificate for his daughter Flóra, stating that she had been too ill in Germany that summer to have travelled back to Hungary. This would provide them with a reason to satisfy the police as to why they had overstayed their visas.

Our suitcases were considerably heavier on our return journey from Braunschweig. There was only one train from East-Berlin to Budapest leaving at 10.30 pm, and the connections were bad – either we would arrive at 9.30 pm at Friedrichstrasse, leaving only an hour to cross the border and get to the Ostbahnhof, or we would arrive at 6 pm, giving us a good four hours. We decided that the possibility of missing the Budapest train and having to wait twenty-four hours for the next was not worth the risk.

At 2 pm we drew out of Braunschweig station and arrived at the last western station, Berlin Zoo, at almost 6 pm. It was dark as the crowds of West Berliners got off the train and headed for the bright neon lights of their city. Some looked at us curiously, one even called through the compartment door, 'This is the last stop in West Berlin!' I thanked him and remained seated. Two elderly ladies sitting opposite, ignoring us, began to chat. 'I'm always so nervous going back, I'll have to go to the loo,' with which she left the compartment.

On crossing the Berlin wall at night, I concluded that the entire East German national grid must be working overtime, lighting up the area like Blackpool illuminations. Guards with dogs patrolled the barbed wire perimeter while others with binoculars watched the train from their look-out towers.

There were fewer people crossing over at Friedrichstrasse than there had been on our westward journey. We stood in line waiting, and watched the pathetic scene as a guard ordered an elderly man to open his brown, battered suitcase. Moving some of the clothes to one side, he withdrew an orange and began to examine it minutely, holding it up to the light. The man waited nervously, fidgeting, passport in hand. Then the guard replaced the orange and motioned to its owner that he was free to close his case and leave.

As western nationals in transit we were of no particular interest, though we were asked about the contents of our suitcases. Back through the 'horse boxes' and up the steps to the S-bahn. Arriving at the Ostbahnhof we found the small waiting room completely full. We had some spare East German marks, weightless as milk bottle tops, and decided to eat in the station restaurant to keep warm and pass the time. It was a cheerless place, its dullness reflected in the tasteless food. Nevertheless, it was busy, and it was with great joy that we heard someone speaking Hungarian at a nearby table from which much laughter emanated.

The train left punctually at 10.30 pm. It had been bitterly cold on the platform and everyone had waited in the tunnel below until the last possible moment. We chatted, finally going to bed in our sleeping compartment at about midnight. We had hardly slept at all when the lights were abruptly snapped on at 12.30 pm. 'Passports, visas!' commanded a voice. We struggled towards consciousness and handed over the various documents. These duly stamped, the East German guard left, to be followed some minutes later by his Czech counterpart. Speaking in German he asked me, 'Where is your Czech visa?'

'There,' I said, pointing to it.

'This is not valid, you have already crossed the border twice,' he continued.

'I don't understand,' I said. 'We live in Budapest and we've been to West Germany and now we're going home. This is what they gave me at the Czech embassy in Budapest.'

'It's not valid,' he repeated.

'Well, can't you sell us a new one?' I asked. 'We've got photos.'

'Maybe when we reach the border in about fifteen

minutes,' he replied. 'You had better get dressed.' So saying, he left the compartment, taking our papers with him.

We dressed and waited. The train soon came to a halt and doors banged as guards disembarked and others got on. Our door swung open. 'You will have to leave the train,' said the guard.

'But why?' I protested. 'Can't you sell us a visa?'

'That is not possible, not until the morning, please bring your belongings.'

We hauled our luggage off the racks and followed him off the train. It was pitch black apart from the lights from the train and bitterly cold with thick snow underfoot. We were led to a small building on the platform and into a large room containing a long, wooden table and chairs. Behind us, the barred gate was locked. We sat down. In the corner of the room a man was asleep, while opposite sat what looked like three Pakistanis. The clock on the wall showed almost one o'clock. After some minutes we heard the sound of a key being turned and a guard came in. 'We can let you have visas at about 5 am when the next shift arrives,' he said. Apparently, there was another train bound for Budapest some time that morning. I translated for Paul, whereupon the three men opposite addressed me. 'We can get visas, five o'clock?'

'Yes,' I replied. 'Where are you going?'

'Islamabad,' came the reply. 'We had luggage stolen in Amsterdam,' they continued, 'but have money and papers.' I nodded.

We lay down along the row of wooden seats, but with the bright lights, the chattering of our companions and noises of the guards in an adjoining room, sleep was impossible. Eventually, at 4.30 am the guard came in again. 'We can't let you have the visas here,' he told us. 'You must go back to West Berlin.'

'West Berlin?' Paul echoed.

'Here's the address,' said the guard, handing me a piece of paper. Protests were in vain, we were to be put on the train coming from Budapest at 5 am. I translated for the Pakistanis.

'Is big trouble?' they asked me.

Is very big trouble,' I replied.

'East Berlin, West Berlin same?' they enquired.

I shook my head.

At five o'clock we were all escorted to the waiting train, including the man who had slept soundly throughout the night's disturbances. The Pakistanis tagged along behind, seemingly unconcerned about what to them was a small detour in a much longer journey. Within minutes the East German guard burst into our compartment. 'Visas! Passports!' he shouted.

'We haven't got visas,' I said wearily, imagining a situation where we could spend an indefinite amount of time sitting on this bleak border. I explained the situation.

The guard leapt to attention, 'We in the German Democratic Republic will give you a visa at any time,' he said, thrusting the familiar forms at me. At 8 a.m. we were back at the Ostbahnhof for the second time in twelve hours. Having decided to leave our cases in the left-luggage, we bought the S-bahn tickets, and with a feeling of being back in my school-teacher days in England I gave each of the Pakistanis theirs, 'One for you, one for you...this way,' I said as they followed in a single file.

Once more through the prefabricated building at Friedrichstrasse, trying to avoid looking at my reflected washed out face and dark-circled eyes under the hard fluorescent lights. Then out into the unknown, the West Berlin tube network, with only the address on the paper we had been given. No-one I approached had heard of the street, and looking at my watch I saw it was already 9.30 a.m, and I realised that few consular departments in embassies would stay open much beyond 11 or maybe 12 a.m. Time passed, and then eventually an old man peered at the address, thought and said, 'Ah yes, I know it, but it's not here, it's over in East Berlin.' We could not believe it, but he was certain.

'What do we do now?' I asked Paul. 'If we don't get to the Czech embassy before they close we'll have to spend the night here and we haven't enough money left.'

'Let's find a phone box and look in the telephone directory in case there's also a Czech embassy here in West Berlin,' he replied. We trooped up onto the street, and not far away was a phonebox, but no Czech embassy was listed.

'What now?' I asked.

'Let's try the British Embassy. They might know,' Paul said.

I relayed the situation to the Pakistanis waiting outside. 'We have friend, West Berlin,' they said after some discussion. 'We go there,' and then with smiles and handshakes they left.

The British Consulate informed us that there was a Czech mission in West Berlin and dictated the address. They also said that the consular department was likely to be open only until 11 a.m. It was already nearly half past ten. We hailed the first passing taxi deciding that our visas were more important than food, and managed to arrive in time to be the last people issued with Czech visas that morning.

With the relief of knowing we could return to Budapest on that night's train, came a sudden and overpowering sense of sleepiness and fatigue. We had not slept since getting up the previous morning in Braunschweig, some twenty-eight hours ago, and there would be no real opportunity to sleep for almost another twelve hours. We decided to remain in West Berlin until evening, though we had no idea what to do with no money and in sub-zero temperatures. We walked the crowded shopping streets, unwashed and unkempt, too tired to talk or even care which direction we were going. Then ahead of us we saw a large, modern church and decided to go inside and have a look. It was warm and dark inside, the Christmas tree still in place, and a few small groups of people admiring the nativity scene and candles. This, then, was the answer. We found two seats behind a pillar, and settling ourselves down, managed to doze on and off for several hours.

Early in the evening we made our way to Friedrichstrasse. 'Where is your luggage?' asked the custom's officer.

'At the Ostbahnhof,' I replied wearily.

'I must see it,' came the response.

'You did – yesterday.'

'I must see your luggage,' he repeated, pointlessly.

I began to explain, slowly, waiting for him to realise that our luggage could only have got to the Ostbahnhof through this same border, when he cut me short and told us to go. My initial feelings of intimidation when we had first crossed through Berlin two weeks earlier were fast turning to impatience and disdain.

Once at the Ostbahnhof, we managed to find two seats in the waiting room and tried not to sleep for fear of losing our luggage. Eventually we boarded the train, now with no booked sleeping compartment or seats – we had been extremely lucky that our tickets had not been punched on our previous day's abortive journey. However, the train was almost empty, and the seats pulled out, so that by pulling out all six we contrived a very comfortable bed.

We crossed the Czech-Hungarian border early in the afternoon and as I stared out of the window I realised that Miklós and János would probably have been to Keleti station the previous day to meet us, and that I was supposed to be teaching that very evening. It was too late to wander the streets in search of a phone that worked. We took a taxi the short distance to our flat and fell straight into bed.

★ ★ ★ ★ ★

1983, and the snow mounds began to melt at the sides of the road, the drains filled to overflowing and simply walking down the street took on an aspect of Russian roulette. The road was a lake of dirty, melting slush from which you were drenched by passing cars and buses, whereas hugging the walls of the buildings left you vulnerable to avalanches of melting snow sliding off the rooftops.

Daily life resumed its pattern of teaching and seeing friends. The days became longer and the eager anticipation of the coming spring was almost tangible. The combination of dark, cold days and the general lack of fresh fruit and vegetables in winter caused Hungarians to yearn for any sign of spring's arrival, to deliver them from what they called 'winter tiredness'. Spring, when it does come, is a sudden eruption. Temperatures rise by ten degrees, the sun shines all day, stalls fill with the smells and colours of spring flowers and vegetables, and winter clothes are put out of sight in the firm knowledge that this is it.

Following the arrival of spring (always dated from March 15th, the national holiday marking the anniversary of the 1848 Hungarian uprising against the Austrians) there is a gradual but relentless increase in temperature right through to July. August gives way to the annual 'Indian summer' of September when days are still like summer but cooler mornings and evenings herald the arrival of autumn. The change from autumn to winter is often as dramatic as that from winter to spring, each season usually being quite clearly distinguished from the next.

Back at home the whimsical gas water-heater in the bathroom refused to light. Having learnt that in such situations it is best to ask a friend to recommend someone to mend it, I mentioned it in passing to our doctor neighbour a few days later. He said he would arrange something and we imagined he would let us know within a few days. Thus, we were dumbfounded to find two gas men on our doorstep at 8 a.m. the following morning. They marched straight into the bathroom, mended the heater in a matter of minutes and then made to leave. I quickly rummaged for my purse in my bag but they categorically refused the proffered note. It turned out that our surgeon neighbour had operated on their boss's leg and he had strictly instructed his workmen not to accept any payment.

A few days later I came home to find Éva waiting for us. Communication was limited, since she spoke no English and my Hungarian was extremely basic. As far as I could understand she was telling me that we would have to leave the flat, it was something to do with the gas, but this I could not follow. Soon Paul was home too, and with the aid of a dictionary we discovered what the problem was. Péter and Éva's flat belonged to the council, which was responsible for the upkeep of both the outside and inside of flats, apart from their decoration. Éva wanted new gas pipes taken into the kitchen for hot water, along with some other modernisations which the council would complete at no cost. But it seemed that Éva had just been told that from the beginning of May tenants would be required to pay half the cost of such work, and they therefore wanted to have it done in April. Since we could not live in the flat while the work was being done, and since Péter would be returning from England in June or July, we decided we should find a new flat to rent from April onwards.

As yet we had not had to flat-hunt in Budapest. Miklós had made all the arrangements with Péter for his flat while we were still in England. We knew there was an acute shortage of housing in the city and yet in seeming paradox, a large number of empty flats. Council flats, which constituted the vast majority of housing, could be inherited. They could also be reclaimed by the council if a person died with no-one else registered as living there. Thus, every child in Budapest is registered as living with a grandparent or other relative, entitling him to inherit the flat when the grandparent dies. In many cases, the grandparent dies while the child is still at school, so the flat remains empty until needed. So it was that thousands of empty council flats existed in a city where you could not even put your name on a waiting list until you had worked for five years, and where you would then in all probability have to wait a further ten or fifteen years before finally being offered a place to live. Many young couples are thus forced to live in their parents' or parents-in-law's flat, and it is not uncommon to find three generations living together, in the best cases with each generation in a separate room, but commonly with grandparents in one room, and their children and grandchildren sharing the other room. Few flats were rented out since the law favoured the rights of the tenant and foreigners were few.

It was also possible to buy freehold flats, but these cost many times the amount needed to secure a council one, and it was a totally impossible option for all but a few. A common, and rather morbid practice, was that of a person making a contract with an elderly person who had no relatives, to inherit their flat when they died. The terms of the contract could vary between paying a lump sum in cash, making monthly payments, or living in the flat of the elderly person and taking care of them until they died. It was thus obviously in the young person's interest to choose as old and as unhealthy a person as possible and hope they would not have to wait long.

One afternoon not long afterwards, Endre called in as he had promised at the time of our first meeting. He was carrying a variety of pipes. 'I've been all over town to get these,' he grinned. 'You can't get them anywhere – they're delivered to the state shops but the assistants sell them at a profit to some small private shop, which automatically doubles the price knowing there are queues of people like me desperate to get them at any price.'

'What are you mending?' I asked.

'The sewer,' he replied, walking in and looking about him. 'Not a bad place,' he said. 'Are you happy here?' We sat down.

'Well, we've got to move actually,' and I told him the situation.

'I might be able to help you,' he replied. 'I know, come over on Saturday and have lunch with us and we'll talk to Kati about it. We may have a place for you.' He wrote down his address on a scrap of paper, refusing the tea I offered to make. 'No, I must go and get on with the sewers, but we'll expect you on Saturday.' Then flashing a characteristic grin he picked up his armful of pipes and left.

On Saturday morning we looked at the map and found we would be able to get to Endre's by walking through the city park, only a fifteen-minute walk from door to door. They lived in a small bungalow with a small, unkempt garden, together with their seven-year-old daughter Flóra and a cat. Smells of fried chicken wafted out from the kitchen window and we were soon seated around the table in the sitting-room. The walls were lined from floor to ceiling with books in various languages, Polish, English, Russian and Hungarian, and magazines were piled on stools and in corners. Conversation soon turned from Kati's and Endre's various jobs of teaching or interpreting to their abortive attempt to defect from Hungary the previous year, and their reasons for wanting to leave. Unlike our other friends, Endre had not a good word to say for the ruling government. 'Everyone's corrupt, the system's corrupt, but it's not that which is so awful, it's that it doesn't work. Everyone's cheating everyone else – you get someone to do a job for you, they overcharge you, you tip them for indifferent work and a week later it's gone wrong again.' I could not help but think of our experience with the removers, where we had been forced to pay and tip someone and then had to move all our things ourselves. He went on in the same vein about the disastrous state of the economy, the total inefficiency of companies, the obstructive bureaucracy, and the corruption and bribery to be found at every level of life, from getting your child into university to buying the few pipes he had needed. Yet he always laughed as if describing something he had read about in another country, and he seemed neither bitter nor depressed.

Their additional month in Germany had cost both of them their jobs, and their passports had been confiscated for four years. 'Oh well,' said Endre, 'it's not the first time. I tried to walk over the border into Yugoslavia when I was sixteen but I was caught. My right to a passport was taken away then too.'

'Endre! We nearly forgot to tell them about the flat!' Kati interrupted. 'We may be able to get a flat for you in Garay

Square – do you know where it is? It's just a few streets away from where you are now. I don't know what condition it's in, it's been empty for years.'

'It belongs to a school friend of mine who's in Canada now,' Endre continued. 'I'll go round and see the old man, her father, this week.'

We chatted until late, agreeing that Endre would drop in with news of the Garay Square flat during the week. He accompanied us back through the park, still deep in conversation about philosophy and politics, gesticulating expansively.

He came, as agreed, a few days later, and suggested he take us to see the flat on the following Sunday. He seemed doubtful that we would want to live there but would not be drawn as to why. But time was short, and as yet no-one else had come up with any concrete possibilities, and somehow, though we had hardly discussed it, Paul and I already knew we would be staying another year. We leaned over the railing and waved to Endre as he crossed the courtyard below. As though he also sensed our unspoken decision he smilingly shouted up, 'You're both crazy, you know that!' We laughed. He was neither the first nor the last to say so. 'Sunday at ten, then! Cheerio!' he called, and disappeared into the deep shadows of the gateway.

Market and May Day
GARAY SQUARE

Endre arrived as planned the following Sunday morning. He tried to prepare us for what we would see in the flat, describing its old furniture and general disorderliness. We were not interested. We had to find somewhere to move within the month.

It may seem strange that Garay Square, a mere two minutes' walk from Dózsa György Street, was completely unknown territory to us. The preceding months from November to April had been spent in such a way that we generally seemed both to leave and return to our flat in the dark. The clocks were put back a month sooner than in England at the end of September and since darkness falls earlier even in the summer months, we had not felt encouraged to explore.

The square was almost silent. It was already warm enough that April not to need a jacket, and the sun shone in our faces as we entered the square. To our left, the Palm Cake Shop was open, its narrow wooden steps divided by a rickety rail enabling two queues to form, one for ice-cream, one for cakes and pastries. The ice-cream queue stretched down the steps and into the street, the people standing dozily in the sun. From the other came a father and son carrying their white parcel of cakes, the cream just beginning to make grease spots on the paper packaging.

Opposite was the main entrance to the market, which was, in fact, Garay Square. The huge, green, wrought iron gates stood padlocked, but outside on the pavement gypsy music could be heard from a transistor radio, coming from one of the many kiosks that surround the market square. The door to the kiosk was open, and outside a dark-haired, dark-eyed woman in her floral nylon apron was sitting heavily on her wooden stool, surrounded by plastic buckets of assorted flowers, and a small blackboard with 'Ferenc' chalked on it, showing that day's name-day. (Every day of the calendar year is associated with one or more Christian names – many were originally a saint's day. While birthdays are usually only celebrated by family and close friends, name-days are also celebrated at places of work and are more 'public' occasions.)

We turned into the square. 'This is it, here,' Endre said. The building was painted a pale lime green; the number above the door was obscured by dirty glass. On the right was a wooden door and next to that a small workshop, the door open and its proprietor sitting in blue, oil-stained overalls, cleaning something I assumed belonged to the car parked by the kerb with its bonnet open and engine running.

We walked into the entrance, bins and letterboxes on either side. It was dark and dusty, the uneven black and white slabs on the floor cracked and dirty. There was an odour of rubbish and damp. We climbed the stone steps to the second floor. Unmistakable smells of fried chicken and coffee came from behind the doors to other flats, with the sound of voices combined with washing-up to the gypsy-music radio programme we had heard outside.

As we reached the top of the stairs the dull, brown door of 'our' flat faced us. Several small brass name-plates announced occupants both abroad and deceased. We rang the bell. After some shuffling and fumbling from within, the door opened to reveal Zoli bácsi. Zoli bácsi: seventy-eight years old, a retired watch-maker whose mother had owned the flat but had died three years previously. Zoli bácsi, who had spent those years doing up the flat for his daughter, resident in Canada with her rabbi husband and children, and who, according to Endre, was never to return.

For a moment he peered at us uncertainly through glasses the thickness of milk bottles – the fate, presumably, of many a watch-maker. Beyond him stretched a long, dark hall, lofty and cool with its high ceiling.

Endre immediately began his usual jolly patter of conversation as we followed Zoli bácsi through the door. The hall had a red flagstone floor and was quite bare except for a tall, carelessly-painted broom cupboard with a dusty spider plant on top. At the far end of the hall were huge double doors with brass handles and glass panels. They led into the enormous main room, with its parquet floor and stucco ceiling. We climbed over the paint tins and newspapers and looked around.

A monstrous chandelier hung from a chain in the centre of the room, grotesque wrought iron looking like something from a Hammer horror film. Below it stood a large, dark dining table with four chairs. The table itself was hidden by an assortment of paint rags, beer bottles, chipped plastic cups, newspapers, pieces of tarnished silver cutlery and paint brushes. The upholstery on the chairs was badly worn; something like straw hung from under the seats of two of them. In one corner of the room stood a black, sarcophagal piece of furniture, its wooden doors open, and crammed for the most part with ancient-looking tablecloths and curtains. The closed glass doors encased vases of dusty plastic roses, yellowing photographs, a few medals and an assortment of keys.

In the opposite corner was a giant dresser with a worn, pink, marble slab over its bottom doors. The drawers were open revealing more tarnished cutlery, plastic spoons and old postcards. Through the glass doors in the top part of the dresser I could see unidentifiable electrical appliances, possibly hotplates and small grills. The marble slab was covered with tools, nails, bits and pieces of clocks, more rags, more paintbrushes and more paint pots.

On a stand by the window a large cheeseplant sat in a white enamel bowl of the kind I was accustomed to seeing in bathrooms for soaking clothes or catching drips from leaking pipes. To our left was the *kályha*, the heating stove, an ornate example and probably valuable, and a television that looked decidedly unlikely to be in working order.

Zoli bácsi stood in the middle of the room, large-boned yet frail, his trousers hanging loosely and his short-sleeved shirt revealing white, sagging arms. The floor was a sea of paint-spattered newspapers, small sticks resting on paint tin lids, and the odd beer bottle or screwdriver put down where it had obviously been last used.

'I've been working here nearly every day for the past three years,' Zoli bácsi informed us, 'painting, fitting the new bathroom. It's my daughter Anna's flat now, they'll be coming to live here when her husband's finished his research in Canada. He's a rabbi you know and Anna's a doctor.' He picked his way over to the open dresser drawer, took out one of the postcards, and raising it till it was perhaps two inches from his glasses, peered at it carefully and then handed it to us. 'This is where they live – I went there last year,' he said.

'Have a look around,' said Endre, resuming his rapid conversation while Zoli bácsi rummaged in the drawer in search, perhaps, of other postcards.

The flat was large. The first door to the left on coming in from outside, led into the kitchen. It had a stone floor, a small wooden table with a peeling plastic covering, the usual double sink unit and small white enamel sink with a cold tap. The cooker was of black cast iron, spattered with whitewash from the newly-decorated walls, the only other thing in the room being a small dresser containing more plastic flowers. Leading off from the kitchen was another room, nearly empty, with a worn rug on the floor, a dusty sofa and two enormous black wardrobes.

Opposite the kitchen, on the other side of the hall, lay the larder, large enough to walk into and bulging with empty bottles, paint tins, glass jars, old flowerpots, chipped crockery and every imaginable kind of rubbish. The toilet was next to that and the bathroom was at the end of the hall. This had obviously also been newly decorated, had a bright blue bathroom suite and tiles, whitewashed walls and patterned blue lino, which had been roughly cut with a bad join in the middle and considerable gaps around the bath and basin. Climbing over the debris in the main room where Endre was still talking, we looked into both the smaller rooms which lay one either side of the sitting room. One had a sofa and a wardrobe. Both rooms had the same nine foot high double doors with brass handles. There was no doubt about how grand the flat had once been.

We stood by one of the windows and looked out across the square. The roofs of the buildings around the perimeter of the market gave way to an open central area full of small, covered stalls and I could make out one or two of the painted signs, 'Live fish and fish soup', 'Poultry', 'Flowers'. There was no sign of life. To the left I could see the cake shop, still with its queue on the wooden steps, and down below I could hear someone relentlessly revving the engine of a car. Then, as I was about to walk away from the window, a movement caught my eye. A cat on the market roof had got up to stretch itself and then lie down again in the sun.

Endre called. 'He says you can have it for five thousand forints a month,' he said. Zoli bácsi stared at us, as if trying to gauge our reaction to the rent. Then he interrupted Endre asking him to tell us that he was not mercenary, he was a good communist and party member but he and his wife were old and still had to pay the council rent for the flat out of their pensions. We told him it was no problem, mentally calculating how many more hours of teaching would be needed to pay the difference between our present rent and this. It was agreed that we could move in on the following Saturday and that by then Zoli bácsi would have cleaned up. Together we again crossed the swathes of paint-covered newspaper and walked to the door. He shook hands with all of us, and almost before we were outside he closed the door and we could hear the sound of the key in the lock.

'Are you sure you can afford it?' asked Endre, as we walked back out into the street and past the shuttered shop windows. 'You'll have to pay the gas and electricity bills on top. I tried to get him to let you have it for four thousand, but he's sharper than he looks. And you don't want to believe all that business about being poor – they've got a lovely flat in Buda, and a summer house up in the hills somewhere.'

We were just relieved that we had somewhere to go, and long after Endre had left us we were still talking about our separate impressions, our plans for earning the rent, reorganising the flat, and the move itself.

The following Saturday morning our friends arrived early. It was already hot. Miklós came in a hired van with a driver, and found us already carrying the first boxes along the balcony and down into the courtyard. It was a slow job even though there were seven of us: Endre, János, Miklós, two friends of his called Kálmán and Jóska, and ourselves. The driver of the van merely loaded the boxes out in the street. One or two people living on the second floor leaned on the railings of the balcony to watch, including an old man in tracksuit trousers and vest, smoking, and a woman in a dressing-gown watering some plants hanging on the wall next to her flat door.

Sometimes we were forced to have a stop in the courtyard between the flower beds, before continuing to the covered entrance, past the letterboxes and bins and out into the street. It was ten o'clock and already 28 degrees. On the kitchen table stood a dozen beer bottles, glasses and an opener, but otherwise the flat was bare.

Endre travelled with the driver to Garay Square while the rest of us carried potplants, the typewriter, the guitar and the bottles. When we arrived they were still trying to park the van, and the man we had seen in the workshop the week before was waving them into the space between two other vans loaded with vegetables. The square was a noisy, swarming multitude of people carrying enormous shopping bags bulging with food from the market, cars hooting, stall-holders shouting and the street was congested with cars, vans and people trying to carry crates and boxes of produce across the narrow road.

There was no time to watch. Endre had already gone up to get the key from the neighbour, and by the time we got there they were inside the flat. She seemed to be an honest, friendly woman and eager to help. We walked to the door of the sitting-room only to find it padlocked, and that the bunch of keys Zoli bácsi had left did not include a key for it. We pooled all the keys we had between us and then tried each in turn: we were in luck, one fitted.

Then began the arduous task of carrying the boxes up the sixty-odd steps to the second floor. In most cases we stopped and sat on the box on the first floor before continuing. All the boxes were dumped in the room next to the kitchen which we had decided we would use to store them when they were empty, and also for any furniture in the other rooms which we did not want.

About half an hour after we arrived, two elderly women walked in through the open door without ringing the bell. Endre appeared to know one of them. She looked critically at us all, and he then introduced us to Rózsi néni (Zoli bácsi's wife) and her sister. Together we walked into the main room which looked considerably transformed. The newspapers and paint tins were gone, though tools and beer bottles still graced the table and marble top of the dresser.

Rózsi néni looked around her as though it had been a long time since she had been in the flat. 'We used to have that room when we were first married,' she said, nodding in the direction of the smaller of the two side rooms. 'Which room are you going to sleep in?' I told her we had decided on the other, larger room, the only problem being that there was no bed. In fact it had only just struck me how bare the sitting room was, with no armchairs or sofa, just the dining table and four dilapidated chairs.

There then ensued a rapid conversation between Rózsi néni and Endre after which he suggested going off in the van to a large second-hand furniture shop and getting a bed. The remaining boxes were off-loaded into the street. The van driver was given instructions how to get to the shop and disappeared with Rózsi néni and her sister. Endre, Paul and I headed for the bus stop telling the others to drink lots of beer and that we would take them all out for a meal when we got back.

Rózsi néni and her sister were already strolling round the 'French' beds when we walked into the shop. It was a cavernous, dark place with brown lino floors and poor lighting, and the furniture was either vinyl or had gaudy floral covers. After looking around and finding a perfectly acceptable bed, the assistant, who was smoking and drinking coffee with the cashier, was summoned. It turned out that the price of the bed included two similarly floral patterned armchairs, so that solved the problem of furnishing the sitting-room. We paid and walked out to the hot, dusty pavement. Endre told us he had to go, he had a job interpreting that afternoon, but organised the van to take us back to Garay Square with the bed and chairs, while the two old women would get a taxi. We were unable to communicate with the driver of the van, and were surprised when he suddenly stopped in a side street near Garay Square. He wound down his window and shouted someone's name. Above us a window opened and a young lad looked out. There followed some more shouted conversation after which the lad emerged from the building and jumped on the back of the van, travelling along sitting in one of the armchairs. The driver smiled at us, and taking his hands off the wheel cupped the biceps of one of his arms with his other hand and pointed to his friend in the back. Then pulling a mock-sour face he squeezed the top of Paul's left arm and grinned. We all laughed and I mimed playing the piano then pointing to Paul, at which he nodded and slapped Paul on the shoulder.

Back in Garay Square only the neighbour was in the flat. The others had left a written message that they would be back in an hour. The boxes were neatly stacked and some beer bottles stood on the kitchen table.

Within minutes we heard the voices of the two women coming up the stairs into the flat. Looking over the railings we saw the two men were just manoeuvring the bed past the dustbins, and were obviously suffering under the weight. We walked back into the flat to find the women trying to decide where the bed should best go. Unfortunately, our opinions differed. Paul, meanwhile, had taken a few hundred forint notes out of his wallet and put them in his pocket where they would be more accessible.

As the men reached the door of the flat their shirts were sticking to them. One of them took his off and hung it on the door handle. Once through the hall and main room the two old women began to give instructions as to where they thought the bed ought to go, while I tried in vain to persuade them to put it elsewhere. Everyone was hot and tired, and the two men were understandably indifferent as to the position of the bed in the room, and impatient with all the contradictory instructions they were being given. Paul, in an outburst of frustration, shouted, 'If only someone could speak English!' at which point the young lad the driver had picked up put his end of the bed down on the floor and said, 'I can speak English, I was born in Northampton.' The van driver looked even more amazed than we did. He obviously had no idea that his friend could speak English. I fetched some beer from the kitchen, the two old women left and the four of us sat on the bed – now exactly where we wanted it. It turned out that the parents of the young man had gone to England in 1956 but by the time their son was thirteen had decided to return to Hungary. He then went to a Hungarian school and had never had any reason to speak English. In fact he spoke well, though hesitantly, searching for words he had not used for years. They finished their drinks, brought up the chairs and, accepting the money as a matter of course, left, deep in conversation.

It was half past one. Our friends had reappeared, so we locked up the flat and walked out into the street. The market gates were open, but only a few stall holders remained, sweeping up cabbage leaves and the odd squashed tomato, and carrying their wooden crates back to their cars   a Volvo, a Mercedes and Ford among them.

Next door, on the other side of our building to the car workshop, was a small café. We looked at the menu in the window but decided against it. We wandered down the road past a shop full of a vast range of sieves and winepresses, a shop selling what was described as 'colonial' furniture and on to the corner. On the opposite side of the road was another possibility called 'The Family Circle'. Outside on the pavement sat a man, a beer bottle to his mouth. Another man in faded blue trousers and vest, his paunch hanging well over his black belt, stood with a woman of indeterminable age, with dyed carrot hair, platform shoes, smoking. The others seemed dubious, but Miklós led the way through the door. Noise and smoke filled the air. The first area we walked into had a long bar with a sink at one end, stacks of glasses piled high, and many smaller bar tops of chest height dotted about, at which people were standing and drinking. The floor was stone and covered with matches, cigarette ends and beer. People were laughing raucously, shouting and gesticulating. To one side was a thick curtain which we pushed through to get to the dining area. This too had a stone floor, small tables and red, vinyl covered chairs. It was marginally less smoky and noisy and in the corner were two empty tables which we quickly pushed together. The waiter arrived, clad as in every restaurant in dark trousers, a white shirt and bow tie.

The food was excellent, fried beef with a mountain of onions and potatoes. We seemed to attract a certain amount of attention, possibly due to the language, probably also because the others were regulars. A sound of shouting and broken glass came from the other side of the curtain. No-one around us took any notice. We paid and left, pushing our way as quickly and unobtrusively as possible past what looked like becoming a nasty argument. A moment after the last of us got out through the door, the bartender hustled a customer, cursing and shouting, out on to the pavement. He began to explain his situation to the man we had passed on our way in, who was still sitting there, and then turned around and swaggered back in.

We crossed back over the road and thanked our friends for their help. There was a sudden shrieking and yelling and this time the customer who had already been ejected once, was pushed out again not only by the bartender but by the waiter too. By one hand he was pulling a fat middle-aged woman in a stained dress by her long, greying hair. They stumbled across the road, he still shouting at the bartender and waiter who had remained standing on the pavement, she shrieking at him. For a moment it seemed as if the man was going back again, when a police car rounded the corner and stopped outside. The man and woman then shambled off, while the man still sitting drinking on the pavement began to fumble in his pockets for his identity card.

All the others left except the twins, Kálmán and Jóska, who seemed to have nowhere special to go, and so returned to the flat with us. We unpacked our bedding and the necessary items to make breakfast with, and we then had our first really close look around all the rooms. Kálmán soon disappeared to his regular haunt, the 'Melodia' disco, while Jóska helped us take down the chandelier which seemed to cast a pall of gloom over the whole sitting-room. It was thick with dust and enormously heavy, and as Paul helped Jóska carry it through to the room by the kitchen I wondered what Zoli bácsi would say if one day he came to the flat. I took a few stray bottles and odds and ends to the larder to join all the other rubbish that lined its shelves.

It began to get dark. Jóska left, and we sat in our newly acquired, though far from new, armchairs and planned to remove the 'sarcophagus' from the room the next day. There were no bookshelves, so finding some would be a priority.

There were no curtains in the flat, and as we passed the window a movement caught our attention. An old woman was walking very slowly on the opposite side of the road, in a long coat of no particular colour, carrying a long pole in one hand, and a vinyl holdall in the other. As she reached the side-gate to the market, she called softly, looking around her almost guiltily. She put her bag on the ground, removed several pieces of cardboard from it and put food onto each one. The cats were already waiting. Taking the pole she pushed the pieces of card under the gate. She waited, maybe to see how many cats had come, quietly talking to them. Then, taking her pole and bag, she shuffled off back down the street.

Sunday, just one week since we had first come to see the flat. We hardly knew where to start. The sarcophagus was to be moved to the back room, but the back room was full of our boxes. In retrospect we realised it would have been better to put the boxes in the other small room.

The doorbell rang. Endre and his wife Kati had come to see how the remainder of the move had gone, and to help us clean up. Kati opened the doors of various cupboards and looked horrified   more newspapers, more bottles, corks, paintbrushes and ancient electrical appliances. She disappeared into the bathroom and re-emerged wearing a faded, baggy tracksuit she had brought with her, and immediately put us all to work removing the rubbish, while she washed out the drawers and cupboards and then started on the floor. So we continued till noon, whereupon we gratefully accepted their invitation to lunch, having lost our previous enthusiasm for moving the boxes yet again. Kati only began cooking when we got back, so while Endre and Paul talked politics, I sat in the garden with their daughter Flóra, half-dozing in the sun. Lunch was late in the afternoon, and it was nearly ten o'clock by the time we had walked through the park and found ourselves back in Garay Square. The Family Circle was closed, but we just caught sight of the cat-woman, as we had come to call her, disappearing round the far corner of the square.

Within a week we had made the major changes to the flat we had planned. The sarcophagus was moved out – almost a day's work, which had meant shifting all the boxes. Bookshelves were found, bought and transported home. Kálmán came and painted the stone flags in the hall and the cupboard in the kitchen. The table in the sitting-room was placed next to the window, the giant cheese plant near the door was moved into the hall, records, books and crockery unpacked, curtain material bought and taken to be made up, a carpet found and most things cleaned. There was no washing machine and the price of a new one was beyond us, considering the increased amount of rent to pay. The tiny fridge was inadequate, but Kati said they were on the point of buying a new one and offered to swap theirs for a couple of old, Indian skirts I had. Endre said he would go back with me to the second-hand shop where we had got the bed, as they also had washing machines.

A few days later we met outside the shop. We walked past the rows of beds and chairs to some stairs that led down to the basement. There were maybe thirty washing machines standing at one end of the room, and a young assistant of about twenty, smoking nearby. Endre walked up to him and began to chat, so I wandered around the machines looking at the prices. Some certainly looked less battered than others, but otherwise there was no way of ascertaining their ages or how long they could be expected to last.

'Have you found one?' Endre asked me. I told him that apart from the price I had no idea which to choose, so after a quick consultation with the assistant, I was shown a particular one that looked neither better nor worse than the rest, and which at 5,500 forints I could just afford. A contract was filled in and a guarantee for three months, after which the assistant disappeared, and we slowly walked upstairs.

At the far end was the desk, surrounded by people filling in forms, or just sitting waiting. We sat down on a nearby bed. Eventually our assistant appeared, handed us various papers and motioned to us to go to the cash desk to pay. As our turn approached I took out the money, then looking at the receipt I saw it said only 4,500 forints, and not 5,500. Endre anticipated my question. '500 for us and 500 for him,' he said. I had no idea what he was talking about. I paid 4,500 and left the shop with Endre. Outside on the pavement stood our assistant with the washing machine. He had already hailed a taxi-van for us, and after a brief exchange I saw Endre hand over a 500 forint note as they shook hands. It was really quite simple: the price on the washing machine was changed to 4,500; I had saved 500 forints while the assistant had made 500. Not bad for ten minutes' work. When we arrived at Garay Square, Paul was looking out of the window and came down to help carry the machine. We put it in the bathroom where there was already an attachment, with the outflow pipe hooked over the side of the bath. Endre left and I collected a pile of washing and put it in the machine, meanwhile explaining to Paul about the money. I switched it on; nothing happened; it was quite dead.

As luck would have it, the state repair shop for household appliances, *Gelka*, had a branch just off Garay Square. This was Paul's destination the following morning, as he left, contract in hand, to set about getting our machine repaired. However, it was naive of us to have expected anything to be so simple. As the woman pointed out, that shop dealt with the 14th district and we were living in the 7th, so Paul would have to go to a different address which she wrote down for him. Twenty minutes later he arrived at the new address, only to be informed that they dealt only with televisions, radio, vacuum cleaner repairs and the like, but they would give him the address of where he had to go. Off he set once again, and found the street written on the scrap of paper in his hand: No. 23 was the Gelka shop. However, on approaching, from the opposite side of the road, it was quite obvious that No.23 was nothing other than a butcher's. Paul walked back and forth – maybe there was a 23/a, or 23/b? Finally, summoning up what reserves of patience he still had, he went and joined the queue of women inside. The smell of cooking sausages and grilled chicken filled the tiny shop. There were several counters in the middle, at which men in blue overalls were standing, grease dripping from their calloused fingers, sausage, mustard and a hunk of bread before them.

'What's it for, *pörkölt*?' shouted the butcher.

'Yes... no, not that piece. Haven't you got anything nicer? What about that there?'

'That's one and a half kilos.'

'Mmmm.. perhaps a chicken. Have you got a nice chicken?'

The butcher unceremoniously picked up one of the pile of chickens and slapped it down on the paper. 'That's a beauty,' he said wrapping it up before any further discussion could ensue. 'One hundred and ten forints.' The woman, still peering unconvincedly at the paper parcel in front of her, opened her purse, while the butcher turned to Paul.

'Er...I'm looking for the *Gelka* service shop,' he said. The butcher merely raised his eyebrows. 'This is No. 23 isn't it?'

'Yes.'

'Well, I was sent here to this address...do you know where it is?'

The butcher shook his head. Paul hurried out past the woman standing in the doorway, prodding the half-unwrapped chicken in her bag. He walked further along the street, and then caught sight of the Gelka sign on the other side.

'Yes?' said the woman sitting on the brown vinyl chair at the desk.

'I'd like to have my washing machine repaired.'

'Address?'

'7th district,' he paused waiting for the inevitable.

'Yes?'

'Garay Square.'

'What's wrong with it?'

'It doesn't go. It's quite dead.'

'Name?'

'Merrick,' he said in as Hungarian a way as the name would allow.

'Tomorrow alright? Between 8 am and 3 pm.'

'Very good. Thank you. Goodbye.'

It all seemed too easy, and we both suspected that no-one would turn up, but they did, and the small electrical fault was soon repaired. It was not the last time the repair man was to call. In the months that followed we had two floods and numerous other problems and finally we were told the necessary spare part was unavailable. It remained unavailable until we left the flat – and the machine – behind some eighteen months later.

★ ★ ★ ★ ★

After perhaps three weeks of living in Garay Square we had a surprise visit. It was early evening when the doorbell rang, and standing outside was an elderly couple; a thin, smiling man, and his plump, beaming wife. He spoke a little broken English, and asked if they could come in. I led them along the hall to the main room, aware of their stares.

'Very nice. How nice you're making the flat,' the man said. His wife just continued to beam silently. Paul came into the room and the man held out his hand and introduced himself. 'We are relatives of Rózsi néni – but please don't tell her we were here – a family difficulty...' We nodded as if we understood. He rambled on about English football teams and his holiday in England some twenty years previously, interspersing these reminiscences with more compliments on the flat, until I wondered if they had come out of pure curiosity just to see it and us. Then, finally, he came to the point. He and his wife were going to Austria on holiday that summer and   as we must surely know   it was very difficult for Hungarians to obtain hard currency, so they wanted to change some money with us. We were completely taken aback. Not even our oldest friends had asked us this, knowing that our earnings were in forints, and that we needed what currency we could get just as they did. And this smiling pair of strangers had sought us out and were expecting us to give it to them. We hastily explained the situation, agreeing to change ten pounds as the only way we could think of getting rid of them. The man pulled the newspaper out of his pocket to calculate the amount, not offering as anyone else in the same situation always would a higher rate of exchange. Then still beaming, and with a last final comment on the transformation of the flat and a promise of a postcard from Austria, they left.

We received the postcard, and unfortunately, several more visits. However, on each occasion we sadly confessed to having no currency, but promised to contact them if any friend or relative were to visit. Once we caught sight of them coming around the square. It was early evening, and heavy drops of rain were already falling from the storm that was to follow. Quickly switching off all the lights and locking the front door we waited to see if they were coming to us. After repeatedly ringing the bell they left a note: 'If you have any news for us, please ring. Kindest regards...'

They never found us in after that, though we had a postcard from Italy and one from Germany. Later, after we left Garay Square, feeling we had escaped their visits for ever, the porter of the Music Academy informed Paul that a man had been calling regularly to ask for our new address, and from his description there was no doubt as to who it was. But apart from once finding ourselves in the same greengrocer's, and having to make a rapid exit, we never saw them again.

Meanwhile, we were having problems with Zoli bácsi. It seemed that after three years of coming to the flat to paint and tinker, he was unable to keep away. Several times after being out, we would return to find the huge cheese plant back in the small bedroom where it had been when we took over the flat. He had also usually watered it, short-sightedly sloshing water and soil on the floor. Once or twice he was just leaving the flat when we arrived home and informed us that he had been repairing something. As we expected, he complained about our having moved the chandelier and furniture and insisted on our moving all our boxes down to the cellar. The last straw came when, at 8 am on a Sunday morning, we got up to find him kneeling in the toilet re-affixing the toilet-roll holder to the wall. We decided to visit Endre and ask him to have a talk with the old man.

We were still not officially registered in the flat. Within a few days of having moved in, a woman had come from one of the travel agencies that also dealt with the renting of flats – – they always charged a far higher rent than was normally agreed privately between landlord and tenant. Either Zoli bácsi had thought of the idea himself or one of his family had put him up to it, but in any event she had arrived while the place was still in an awful mess. After a cursory glance she asked us with disbelief if we were satisfied with the flat, declaring it to be below even their fourth category. We were relieved: the rent would not be going up.

Zoli bácsi arrived one day asking Paul to accompany him to the council offices so that we could be registered. This was in fact entirely superfluous, but he seemed to have an exaggerated fear of, or respect for, authority. When they arrived at the building the relevant office was closed for lunch, so Zoli bácsi invited Paul for a coffee in the large expresso bar in the Emke hotel on the corner. Feeling hungry, Paul ordered an egg mayonnaise for himself as well as the coffee, whereupon Zoli bácsi, much put out, announced that he had only invited Paul for a coffee – 8 forints – and the egg – 16 forints – he would have to pay for himself. The waitress arrived. Zoli bácsi paid for the two coffees, but as the girl could not change the only note Paul had, Zoli bácsi was forced to pay for the egg too. He did so, grudgingly, reminding Paul that he must reimburse him the next time they met.

The extraordinarily hot, dry weather continued into May. Towards the end of the month we received a card from Sue and Steve in Cambridge saying that their first baby, Tim, had been born on the 10th. We decided to send them a telegram. Sue was my oldest friend, we had met at the age of nine at primary school and she and Steve were looking after our piano and cat.

I went to the main post office at Nyugati station on the assumption that sending telegrams abroad would be run-of-the-mill for them. Although countless forms exist for anything from registered parcels to customs declaration forms, none is readily available. Two equally unattractive options exist to obtain one. Either you join the end of a long queue, get the form, fill it in and rejoin the even longer line of people, or apologising profusely for your very existence, you push to the front saying, 'Please forgive me, please be so very kind as to let me have a telegram form,' and then, 'thank you, thank you so much,' as it is unceremoniously shoved towards you. I always refused to ingratiate myself in such a pointless and absurd fashion, so I joined the queue. (When I later asked at the post office why the forms could not be put around the walls for customers, it was explained that people stole them. For what unimaginable purpose I was not told.)

I duly wrote my message and waited until I was once again at the front of the queue. I pushed the form towards the unsmiling woman behind the curtained widows. After a cursory look at it she pushed it back.

'I can't send this,' she said.

'Why not?' I asked incredulously.

'Because there's no such place as this in England,' she stated, in a matter-of-fact voice. For a moment I was dumbfounded.

'But there is, I've been there,' I said unconvincingly.

'No. Not in England. In America, yes Cambridge,

Massachusetts, but not in England.'

'But there was a Cambridge in England long before there was one in America,' I spluttered.

The woman sighed. She opened a tome to her left and leafed through it. 'See?' she said, pointing to the word CAMBRIDGE. 'In America.'

Luckily, the man standing behind me in the queue, obviously identifying my accent, decided to help. 'Surely she knows where it is, she's English,' he said.

The woman, now outnumbered, decided on a conditional surrender. 'Alright, I'll send it,' she said, 'but on one condition. You have no right to your money back if we can't deliver it. You'll have to sign here to say that you take the responsibility.'

'I'll risk it,' I replied, the irony lost on her completely. I duly signed the form and left the building with the same degree of bemusement Alice must have felt on leaving the Mad Hatter's Tea Party.

★ ★ ★ ★ ★

Six weeks after we had moved in my mother came from England for a holiday. I had opted out of most of my teaching commitments for those two weeks, though there were one or two lessons I could not find anyone to substitute. It was after an afternoon of teaching that I returned to the sound of raised voices as I opened the door to the flat. Walking into the room I saw a small circle of chairs, and sitting there was Rózsi néni, looking quite unmoved by the shouting, Paul looking worried, my bewildered mother – unable to understand a word – and Zoli bácsi, extremely agitated. In the middle stood Endre, pacing back and forth, gesticulating expansively and giving me only the merest hint of a smile before continuing with his speech. The others were so riveted they hardly seemed to notice that I had arrived. Apart from a few outbursts from Zoli bácsi, Endre continued unabated for maybe fifteen minutes, stopping only once to grin at my mother and say in English, 'Don't worry, it'll all be okay,' before continuing his vehement argument.

I sat down next to my mother who whispered that this had been going on since half past one. I glanced at my watch: just past three o'clock. About fifteen minutes later Endre seemed to be reaching some kind of conclusion, and reluctantly Zoli bácsi and Rózsi néni got up to leave.

Endre saw them out and returned, all smiles. 'What was all that about?' I asked.

'Zoli bácsi says we've got to leave the flat,' said Paul.

'Why?'

'Don't worry, you don't have to leave,' said Endre, 'but I think you should have something in writing. I've told him he's got a month to make up his mind, and then we'll make out a contract for a year. But don't worry, they wouldn't want to give up the money.'

Little by little the main points of the conversation were repeated to me. The most extraordinary factor was that Zoli bácsi had mentioned the possibility of getting divorced from Rózsi néni and coming to live in the flat. He was 78, she 76, and he could hardly walk up the stairs from the street. He was frail and could hardly see and it would be quite impossible for him to manage alone.

As usual, Endre was right. A month later they returned and signed the contract Endre had prepared. No mention was made of divorce, and Zoli bácsi agreed to come to the flat only to collect the rent. As they left our neighbour passed the door and exchanged a few words with Rózsi néni. Zoli bácsi hung back in the hall and took Paul to one side. I heard him say softly, 'It's my wife who doesn't want you to stay here, not me.' Then shaking Paul by the hand, he joined Rózsi néni and they slowly made their way down the stairs.

Garay Square and its surrounding area was commonly known as 'Chicago'. When I told anyone that we were living there, they greeted the information with surprise and distaste.

It had become a focal point for Poles, gypsies, alcoholics, tramps and dubious business. A large supermarket bordered one side of the market, and it was there that the Poles gathered. After their arrival at Keleti station nearby, they carried their assorted bags and suitcases of bric-a-brac to sell outside the market. It seemed that literally anything could be bought and sold there – bottles of cognac, second-hand underwear, clothes, furs, old shoes and boots, quartz watches, baskets, broken toys and dolls, leather jackets, deodorant sprays – anything at all. Bargains were struck in the dust on car bonnets Prices written then erased and a lower price drawn, only to be crossed out again, and so on, until a final amount was agreed. Then they spent their forints on food, and carried their laden suitcases back to Keleti station. Often there were so many of them that getting in and out of the supermarket was all but impossible. More than once someone wanted to buy my shopping bag as I fought my way through the crowd.

The alcoholics and tramps congregated just inside the main gate to the market. They seemed to spend the greater part of every day collecting cardboard which could either be sold or used for bedding. They sat, often quarrelling loudly, next to the window where empty deposit bottles were returned to the supermarket. As the market was locked at night they obviously did not sleep there. Maybe they slept in the cellars of surrounding buildings, but when the market was open they were there, and I came to recognise them. One man with two walking sticks I had frequently seen sitting begging in the underpass at Keleti station. But here in Garay Square, leaving his sticks with his compatriots outside, he strolled into the supermarket filling his basket with bottles of beer.

Somehow, the women were a more disturbing sight than the men. They looked dirtier, quarrelled and even fought more, and I wondered what chain of events had led them here.

Further inside the gateway were the gypsies, mainly women and their teenage daughters sitting on the ground, wearing huge skirts and gaudily coloured headscarves and aprons, and surrounded by babies and young children. They offered quartz watches and watch batteries for sale, calling to anyone passing while continuing to breast-feed children anywhere up to the age of five.

Inside, the main area of the market consisted of fruit, vegetable and meat stalls. These were supplemented with a fish stall selling carp and fish soup – delicious if you have patience and are not too hungry to pick your way through the hundreds of bones (sea fish is unknown, Hungary being a landlocked country); a mushroom stall where people who had picked their own can have them examined and are given a certificate declaring them safe, which is always displayed alongside the mushrooms; a small shop selling beer, wine, soft drinks and tins of food where I found the only tinned salmon of our stay, and a small shop with everything from French perfumes and Scotch to bottles of Heinz ketchup and Worcestershire sauce.

The majority of the stalls were supplied by various state-owned enterprises, but around the perimeter were smaller stalls and tables behind which sat people from the countryside with leathery, brown hands, and deeply wrinkled faces. Men in leather waistcoats, long boots and hats, and women in multitudinous petticoats and headscarves. Their produce was usually of better quality and slightly more expensive, and was carefully laid out before them: a basket of eggs (free range), a chicken, maybe a duck, jars of honey, small bunches of parsley carefully tied up, carrots, yellow paprika – all types of vegetables and fruit according to the season.

It took us a while to adapt our cooking to the seasons, after the availability of everything all the year round in England. The drop in price at the peak of the season was also something unknown to us: tomatoes for example, in March and April cost a good 300 forints for a kilo, but by September they were 6 forints.

A small covered area of the market was given over to stalls of flowers and plants which people brought from their gardens.

From the windows of our flat the whole square was spread before us. While we ate breakfast we could see the throngs of Poles bargaining outside the market, the gypsies inside, the loading, unloading, and the queue on the steps of the Palm cake shop. Occassionally the crowd of Poles would disperse, some into the market, some into the supermarket, while some strolled off down the road. Others gazed nonchalantly into a nearby shop window, pointing things out to the person standing next to them. Then, from the far corner of the square, two policemen would saunter past the supermarket and occasionally through the main gate, but it was rare that they caught anyone. If they did, it was usually because they had come by car, and obviously whatever method of signalling a police presence operated in the square, it could not be carried out fast enough.

Our neighbour, Feri bácsi, a retired coach driver, was almost as permanent a fixture on one corner of the square as the phone box was on the other. He would happily stand and watch the comings and goings from after breakfast until lunch, while in the afternoons he was frequently to be seen attending to his newly-acquired Skoda parked nearby. Or he would lean on the bonnet of the car parked outside Imre's workshop while Imre himself, oily rag in hand, continued to clean some spare-part, nodding every now and then as Feri bácsi held forth. They were known to everyone on the square and knew everyone, so it came as no surprise to us (though it amazed those involved) when someone trying to find us asked a person standing in the street, 'Where do the English people live?' and they received the immediate reply with outstretched arm, 'Up there'.

★ ★ ★ ★ ★

The flat became hotter and hotter as May turned into June, and we began to make plans for going home for the summer. We had to hand in our identity cards and passports in order to obtain our exit visas. It seemed strange, that, like Hungarians, we could not leave the country without exit visas, costing us 400 forints each for the privilege.

Next we found the British Airways office to buy our tickets. 'What kind of passport are you travelling on?' asked the immaculately dressed woman behind the desk.

'British,' I replied.

'Well, if you travel before July 1st it will be 157 pounds.'

'I would like to pay in forints.'

'I'm sorry, if you're travelling on a British passport that's not possible.'

'But we work here. We're not attached to the Embassy or anything and we only earn forints.'

She looked unconvinced, but handed me a form and said, 'You should go to the Hungarian National Bank with this, and if they stamp it for you, you can pay in forints. Do you know where it is?' She explained how to get there, and made seat reservations for us.

The National Bank was an imposing building in Szabadság Square dominated by the TV headquarters and the American Embassy. After showing our form to various people, we were directed to a window where no-one else was standing. We began trying to explain our predicament. The woman turned the form over and over shaking her head, while asking us to produce our I.D. cards. We explained that we had had to hand them in to get our visas. She smiled and shook her head again, it was obvious that there was no point continuing this until we had our papers back.

Some days later, after repeated phone calls to KEOKH (the office dealing with foreigners), we had our visas, I.D. cards and passports back. This time a man was sitting behind the glass at the bank, and it appeared he had never seen such a form before. He read it carefully, then disappeared with it for some ten minutes before returning and saying he could not stamp it for us.

Time was getting short. We should already have paid for our tickets and if they now refused to allow us to pay in forints, it would take us still more time to get enough hard currency together. We went back to the Academy where we were obligingly given a photocopy of Paul's contract and a covering letter, but these were also rejected. The man at the bank then asked if we had tried the main police station, so mentally writing off the rest of the day, we thanked him and left.

At the main door of the police building stood a policewoman, and it was only after informing her of what you wanted that you were handed a numbered tag, and allowed in. We wandered up to the first floor to find every chair and most available floor-space covered with rucksacks and student-types of various nationalities. The doors along the corridor, which were all shut, had the names of countries above them. After watching and waiting for a short while, it became obvious that no queuing system operated, and due to the large numbers of people it was not even possible to determine who was waiting to go into which room. Scanning the names of the countries above the doors – all in Hungarian of course, many quite unrecognisable: for example Olaszország (Italy), Lengyelország (Poland) we decided that the best ploy was to feign ignorance and go into whichever room seemed least busy.

We tried the handle of the door with several Far-Eastern countries named above it and slowly walked in. The office was unremarkable – a few tables, chairs, lino floor, the smell of coffee, a limp spiderplant in the window and a pall of smoke hanging over everything. 'Yes?' said a man in sandals, an open-neck shirt, coffee glass in one hand, and cigarette in the other.

We began to explain about the form. 'Impossible,' he said, 'I can't do it. If you only have a temporary permit, you have to pay for tickets in hard currency.'

'But we don't earn any!' I protested, and pointing at Paul's contract I continued, 'Look. This is what we earn. We are not here on a grant or with the embassy. We have work-permits and we work here earning forints.'

'I'm sorry. Only those with a permanent resident's permit can buy their tickets in forints.'

'And how can you get one?' I asked.

'If you settle in Hungary.'

'What does that mean? How long do you have to be here for that?'

What it meant was that you had to be married to a Hungarian. Even if we decided to stay for twenty years we could get no other type of permit than the one we had. The man agreed that it was unfair for us, but pointed out that we were a unique case, and rules were made for the majority.

We left, handing back the tag, and made for the Művész Café nearby to decide what to do next. It was cool and airy with marble table-tops, green plush period furniture, waitresses in black skirts with small aprons, and an atmosphere of timelessness. At the table in the corner was a group of maybe eight or nine elderly people, cups of coffee and small glasses of mineral water before them. Some minutes later a newcomer arrived, at which point the men rose, kissed her hand and fetched another chair, while the conversation which revolved around illnesses, doctors and forthcoming holidays, continued. When the waitress had a minute, she went over to them, chatting in a friendly, familiar manner. It was obvious that this same group met here regularly.

At the next table was a man reading a novel, another reading a newspaper and two women bent over a crossword puzzle.

It did not take us very long to decide what we had to do. Miklós liked a problem to solve, and recently had had less to do as our ability to cope with Hungarian improved and we got to know the ropes. I went to ring him.

Fifteen minutes later we got off the tram at Rákóczi Square. There were no girls around, though a couple of men were hanging about outside the flower kiosk on the corner. We groped our way up the dark stairway (we never trusted the lift that lurched and screeched its way up) to the first floor, and went in. Clearing copies of The Herald Tribune and the Economist off the chairs, Miklós sat us down and brought us coffee. Then settling himself in the armchair with a glass of cognac and lighting a cigarette, he said, 'OK. Tell me.'

Paul explained while I helped myself to some of the melon from the bowl on the coffee table. When he had finished, Miklós, stubbing out his Marlboro into an already full ashtray, said, 'There's only one thing I don't understand... Why didn't you come before?'

Then he told us that quite recently he had needed just five dollars to pay someone who had brought a book for him from America, and he was recommended to go and see a woman working as a beautician in one of the hotels. She asked him how many dollars he wanted, to which he had replied 'Five'. Her immediate response was, 'Five hundred, or five thousand?'

It was reasonably cool in the room, the wooden shutters allowing only a few dusky shafts of sunlight through giving a warm, subdued light. It was untidy as usual, illustrating the endless comings and goings with no time to finish one thing before starting the next: magazines, newspapers, letters both opened and unopened on the table, teaching books with hastily-scribbled lesson notes on scraps of paper tucked inside, unmarked pieces of homework, cassette tapes, unwashed coffee cups and glasses, clean clothes in piles on chairs, newspaper cuttings, telephone numbers scrawled on serviettes, and ashtrays balanced on bookshelves. The phone rang, as it did literally every few minutes, and we said goodbye as Miklós pulled out the following week's Lingua timetable from under a heap of newspapers, lit another cigarette and said he would contact us. By the following evening we had the required amount of money in a variety of currencies: dollars, German marks, Swiss francs, Austrian schillings and a few pounds of our own. The next morning at the British Airways office the same woman asked me what currency I would like to pay in.

'Mixed,' I replied.

'How mixed?' she asked.

I put the little heaps of notes of different denominations onto the desk. It must have been obvious how I obtained the money, but quickly calculating the total, she confirmed our reservation and handed me the tickets, no questions asked.

It was towards the end of May that Péter had called in from our previous flat in Dózsa György Square, bringing a letter for us that had been sent to the Vántus Károly address. It was from the embassy. Despite having registered both the Dózsa György Street and the Garay Street addresses, they were still sending things to our first flat, and it was only due to the goodwill of the woman there that she forwarded them to Péter who then brought them to us.

It was an invitation from the Ambassador, printed in black with the royal crest embossed in gold, to a celebration of the Queen's Official Birthday in June. British residents were apparently invited to this event, and never having been to anything similar, we decided to go. It was to be held in the garden of the Ambassador's residence in a very beautiful part of Buda.

We travelled by taxi. The weather was unbearably hot, and the thought of squeezing ourselves on to trolleys and trams full of warm, sweaty bodies was decidedly unappealing. Dressed in suitable 'garden-party' attire, we set off. We crossed the river and started up Rózsadomb, an affluent area, but as we approached the road leading up to the Ambassador's residence we were stopped by police. Ahead of us was a long queue of black shiny limousines, sporting the flags of various of nations, and from behind tinted windows, ambassadors and VIPs waited for their chauffeurs to pull up outside the residence. The taxi driver suggested we walk the last hundred yards, and indeed there was a constant stream of people heading in the same direction on foot. Outside on the pavement stood a long file of men in suits and women in floral creations (one or two even with hats), clutching their invitations and glancing around for a familiar face. We joined the queue and shuffled slowly but steadily towards the door.

It was then that I noticed we were being watched from numerous balconies of flats all around. Hungarians had prepared as carefully for this afternoon as those with invitations. Sitting in shorts and swimming costumes they had arranged tables and chairs on their verandahs, with drinks, snacks (and probably friends invited too), while those without such a vantage point hung gaping from their windows. This spectacle had obviously become an annual event for local residents as much as Royal Ascot Week or Henley Regatta in England. Few people in the queue seemed to have noticed, or perhaps more likely had chosen to try to ignore this goldfish bowl sensation, and pretend the party was every bit as private as one behind the walls of Buckingham Palace.

Invitations were not requested, we simply shook hands with the Ambassador and walked straight on out through the French windows and on to the lawn.

I deliberately use the word 'lawn' since it is an item of such rarity in Hungary. It was already covered with guests who included the Primate of Hungary, Hungary's Chief Rabbi, film directors, Ambassadors from many other embassies and an assortment of top people from various fields. Around the borders of the garden were small tables shaded by parasols, from behind which butler-like looking waiters served a large variety of drinks. Meanwhile, waitresses in black skirts and white aprons circulated inconspicuously, carrying silver platters of assorted savouries on cocktail sticks. One was only enough to identify the taste and to get any more you had either to be brazen enough to take two or three at a time, or swallow one down and grab another before the waitress disappeared. Drinks, on the other hand, were available in unlimited quantity. The imbalance in the intake of alcohol and food creating a noticeable effect in some people after an hour or so. Guests stood in small groups, some chatting relaxedly, drink in hand, others indulging in raucous laughter.

Two hours later, having managed to waylay the waitress only once or twice more, we were feeling hungry and tired of standing. We had met several people we knew, but they too had either left or were leaving. Some Hungarians obviously saw the opportunity to make the acquaintance of someone who might later be useful to them, and hovered on the edge of a little cluster hoping to catch the eye of someone they already knew and be admitted to the group. I had expected some kind of formal toast to the Queen, but no such event seemed to be in prospect, so we made our way back through the elegantly decorated hall, stealing a look at the antique furniture in one or two of the rooms where the doors were open, and then strolled back down the road to the nearest bus stop.

The week of our departure for England arrived. We had decided to leave a letter in the flat for Zoli bácsi's daughter and her husband, who were apparently to visit while we were away. Rózsi néni came to collect the rent, saying Zoli bácsi was ill, and told us that unless her daughter managed to pass the Canadian examinations in medicine, enabling her to work there, they would probably return to Hungary. She was perfectly pleasant, wishing us a good trip home and then, just as we got to the front door she said, 'You know I'd like you to stay here in the flat, you've made it so nice and you're such nice people, but it's my husband – he doesn't want you to stay.' Then she smiled wanly, shrugged her shoulders, and left.

Endre and Kati turned up on the evening before we left. We had decided not to cook but to go out somewhere nearby to eat, and invited them to come with us. Several times I had passed a restaurant on Dózsa György Street called the *Chimneysweep* (Kéményseprő), which had an area with tables outside under the trees. It looked like a place much frequented by locals, usually a guarantee of good food. We walked the short distance, telling Endre of Rózsi néni's visit. 'They'll never come back,' said Kati.

'In Canada they've got a big house, a car, a boat; the children both go to school there and speak fluent English. Can you imagine them leaving all that to come back to Garay Square?' Endre asked scornfully.

The fact that we were fond of Garay Square and the area, was a source of amazement to Endre, not surprisingly, since he had grown up in one of the back streets in a flat consisting of one room and a kitchen, with a key to a bathroom on the outside walkway around the courtyard. This had to be shared with several other families and always froze in the winter. He was frequently to be heard wishing the whole area would be bulldozed to the ground, much preferring the comfortable, though totally characterless, high-rise blocks that had replaced such housing in other areas of the city.

We arrived at the restaurant. It was a large, low, stone building with green, flaking paint on the trelliswork in the 'garden' area. In the middle was a small, round bandstand in which stood a cimbalom, some stools and one or two instrument cases. A few people were eating, and we found ourselves a table surrounded on three sides by vine-covered trelliswork. There was a row of these 'boxes', as they were called, going right round the garden; in one of them two or three tables away, an argument was going on. The waiter brought us the menu and we chose our food and wine, then watched as the gypsy band arrived to play. Kati groaned. Like most Hungarians she found the music irritating, especially because it was usually so loud that it was impossible to hold any kind of conversation. It did not stop Endre however, whose hearty laughter could be heard above the sound of the band.

90

Suddenly, there was a voice behind us and a face peered through at us from the other side of the trellis. It was Endre's mother. She had heard his laugh as she was walking by, but confessed surprised distaste at finding him in 'such a place'. We admitted to having invited them there with us, and pulled up another wooden-slatted chair for her. She declined any food, and pulled out a letter from her bag, asking Endre to translate it for her since it was in Polish. He had to shout to make himself heard, trying at the same time to eat his food while it was still hot.

Meanwhile, the two men who had been arguing nearby had moved over to the bandstand, still shouting at each other. Endre finished translating the letter, but his mother wanted him to write a reply for her in Polish. She too had to shriek to make herself heard and several times shook her head shouting, 'Why do you come to a place like this? Do you really like it?' Endre told her how much we enjoyed living at Garay Square, which seemed to confirm all her worst suspicions.

The food was excellent as I had suspected. But it was true that the Chimneysweep had a rather dubious clientele. The two arguing men were now pushing each other around, heading, unfortunately, in our direction. Watching from the door of the building were two women who could also have been involved in some way. One of the two men had earlier asked the gypsy musicians to play a particular song for them, something which is always tipped. So, not to be done out of their money, the two violinists and the clarinettist followed the scuffling men around the garden, continuing to play the request, just five paces behind. The fight reached us, one man pushing the other backwards on to the table, and we hastily removed our plates and glasses to a safe distance. Endre's mother jumped up and Kati burst out, 'Why do you have to fight here, on our table? Can't you see we're trying to eat? For heaven's sake!' At this they stopped, stood up straight, and said, 'Sorry, sorry, excuse us,' and nodding an apology to us all, walked over to the other side of the garden where they continued their scuffle, still escorted by their serenaders.

Endre's mother gave up and decided to leave, making Endre promise to call in later and complete the letter. We finished eating, paid, and headed for home to finish our packing.

★ ★ ★ ★ ★

July and August were spent in England. Maybe the strangest feeling after a year away was the simple fact that we could understand everything everybody was saying. It was a relief to sink back into automatic reactions to situations, conversations which required no effort, shops where you could buy what you wanted when you needed it and the pervading simplicity of everyday life. Yet after that initial relief followed a restlessness, an irritation with the grey weather, a feeling that life was too easy, too routine, too 'nice.' It lacked the struggle, the intensity and the colour of Hungarian life. It made no demands on the abilities and reserves of character we had only discovered in ourselves during the previous year, and personal relationships seemed weak in a society where everyone could, and did, manage their everyday lives without the help of their friends. Thus it was with mixed feelings of trepidation and excitement that we returned to Budapest at the end of August.

Miklós was there to meet us at the airport, flowers in hand, like most people waiting to meet friends and relatives. It was still as hot, dry and dusty as when we had left. 'So, what do you notice first now that you're back?' asked Miklós, as we pushed our way through the milling throngs around the door leading from the customs hall. 'Three smells,' I replied, 'Hungarian coffee, Hungarian cigarettes and the pollution from the cars.'

We got a taxi from the airport. The grass and shrubs were brown, parched by the continual sunshine and three months without rain. We arrived back at the flat and collected the keys from Manci néni. She had offered to water the plants and bring up our letters from the mailbox while we were away, and it was obvious as soon as we walked in that she had also cleaned the flat for us. Miklós stayed half an hour and had a drink and a cigarette, then left, telling us that Rézi was expecting us to go and eat at their place that evening.

We looked around, nothing had changed. We went through the mail which included a note from Endre saying he would be coming to see us soon, some postcards from both English and Hungarian friends and a few letters. One of the postcards was from someone called Virginia. We were astounded to read that she was from California, had married a Hungarian Calvinist minister whom she had met in Chicago, and had just come to live in Dabas. At the theological college in Chicago she had also met an English friend of ours who had gone there to study – it was he who had given her our address. She was keen to meet us and asked us to write suggesting a possible time. We unpacked some things, opened the blinds and windows and then just stood and gazed at the familiar scene below. There was a knock and the door opened. Manci néni had just baked some doughnuts and invited us to go and have some, so we left our re-acquaintance with the market and went next door.

Their flat had two large rooms and was spotlessly clean and tidy. Colourfully embroidered cushions were piled on chairs and sofa, and every available inch of shelf space was crammed with ornaments and dolls in national costume. Proudly, they showed us a music-box gondola they had bought in Venice which played 'O sole mio'. Their budgie was perched on the standard lamp – they had no children and were absolutely delighted the day that the bird had flown into their kitchen and made itself at home. Its favourite trick was to fly down and perch on Feri bácsi's beer glass and drink from it.

Manci néni brought a large plate piled high with warm doughnuts, along with coffee, tonic water and small savoury scones. They told us that they had had a family to stay with them from East Germany, people they had met the previous year on a campsite there. However, the Germans spoke no word of Hungarian, nor they a word of German, but they laughed and said they had had a good time, and that if it was desperate they always had a dictionary. They told us with pride how amazed the Germans had been at the variety and quantity of fruit and vegetables in the markets. Apparently, the food was the only part of their holiday in East Germany that had been a trial for Manci néni and Feri bácsi. Like all Hungarians travelling abroad though, they had taken a good supply of salami and tinned food with them.

They told us that they had seen Zoli bácsi and Rózsi néni with their daughter and her family, and how wild and spoilt the children were. Though they had not stayed in the flat, we later found our small radio broken, presumably by the children. It seemed that the family were quite happy there, in Canada, and had no objection to our staying in the flat, but had not left any messages for us.

Time was getting on, and Manci néni had to leave for her afternoon job of selling the Budapest evening newspaper near Keleti station. Like most pensioners, they simply would not have been able to manage on their state pension and so supplemented their income however they could. We gave them a few small gifts we had brought from England, and then left to buy some wine and go to Miklós's.

On the corner of Rákóczi Square Paul decided to buy some flowers for Rézi, but I saw Miklós waving and beckoning from his balcony so I went on ahead. Miklós, Rézi and I stood and watched from the balcony as Paul took his flowers and walked towards us. Standing outside the building next door was one of the regular girls – black skirt, satin blouse and handbag slung carelessly over one shoulder – and as Paul approached we saw her go up to him and say something. He paused, shook his head, and looking somewhat embarrassed walked on while the girl sauntered on to the corner.

'Well, how much?' asked Miklós.

'I don't know,' said Paul,

'She just asked me if I wanted to go with her.'

'Oh, you English!' said Miklós in his usual mock-sarcastic way.

On the following day my brother Brian was due to arrive for a two-week holiday with us, so for the second time within 24 hours we were at the airport. While waiting for the plane to land we went to the small post office on the first floor to get a police registration form for him. (It was compulsory for the residence of all visiting foreign nationals to be registered at the local police station.) The airport building was hot and stuffy so we joined the people outside on the roof craning their necks for a better view of the plane. The heat shimmered over the asphalt surface as the jet came in to land.

On the way home we asked the taxi driver to stop at a cake shop and took Brian in to choose some cakes. The flat was stifling when we returned, the dilemma always being whether to keep the windows closed to prevent the hot air coming in, or to have no air at all. We decided that when it had cooled down a little in the evening we would go down to the river and register Brian's arrival at the police station. At about six o'clock it was still 28 degrees, but the sun was going down and it was pleasant to be out. The walls of the buildings radiated warmth and we sank into the tar in places as we crossed the roads.

The police station was not far, and a policeman was sitting in the shady entrance on a wooden chair, smoking and reading the evening paper. He looked up as we walked in, handed us a numbered tag and directed us to the door on the right inside the courtyard. We walked up the few steps, turned to the right and knocked on the door, its pane of glass covered on the inside by a dirty gray net curtain. The office was sparsely furnished with a desk, several wooden chairs, a telephone and a typewriter. In the corner stood a filing cabinet and above it on the wall a map of Budapest with its districts marked in different colours. Next to that was a shelf with a television set tuned in to a football match. We had had to forge Zoli bácsi's signature on the form since he was ill and Rózsi néni was not registered as a tenant of the Garay Square flat. The policeman hardly glanced at it before stamping it, handing back the visa form and passport and bidding us good-evening. Closing the door behind us, we heard voices to the left of the courtyard. In the shadows stood a tall, heavily built gypsy handcuffed to a stout policeman. The gypsy was well dressed, with a white jacket and white shoes, and stood sheepishly leaning against the crumbling wall. The group walked out ahead of us to a waiting police car.

Down by the river smartly-dressed couples strolled along the promenade or sat on one of the many chairs and benches, soaking up the last rays of the sun. The mighty Danube flowed quickly by, reflecting the hill on the far bank, the vast building of the royal castle and the spire of the Matthias coronation church high above. Everywhere along the river were cafés and restaurants, chairs, tables and parasols on the promenade, people chatting, eating, drinking or lazily sauntering past. Later, after dark, the castle church and bridges would be illuminated, and the many lights of steamers would shine back from the water as tourists and locals lingered outside, while lovers and lone fishermen sat on the stone steps leading down to the water's edge and watched the boats go by.

Later, on our way to eat, we heard a voice behind us. 'Hello, what are you doing here?' It was Endre, but before we had a chance to reply he shook my brother by the hand and said, 'If you're not going anywhere special, why don't you all come with me and have a meal? I'm with a group of Poles on a bus tour, but I'm sure we can find room for you.' He led the way to one of the car parks by Keleti station. There was a queue of taxis, the drivers sitting either with their doors open and radios on, or standing chatting and laughing with other drivers. There were students, soldiers and country people carrying enormous loads across the station yard which was full of parked coaches from Poland and Czechoslovakia and one from the Soviet Union.

Endre led us to a rusty green coach with dingy curtains, climbed on and counted heads. One or two were missing: the people who had come to buy and sell in Garay Square. Those already on the coach were showing one another what they had bought, talking animatedly. Endre looked at his watch saying, 'These Poles, always late, always unreliable, they're just like children.' Then from the far end of the station yard, we saw Kati returning from Garay Square. She looked heavenwards and shrugged helplessly as she led a straggling group of chattering Poles back to the bus.

There were some free seats on the coach, and no-one seemed in the least concerned about who we were or why we were there. The coach drove off to their hotel so that Endre could collect the few people who had not gone to Garay, and then we set off for our meal. Animated conversation and laughter continued as the Poles passed their purchases back and forth over the seat backs for their friends to inspect, while Kati used the microphone to describe the trip.

The restaurant was on the outskirts of the city and had a large garden. We were met at the gate by the head waiter dressed in traditional folk costume, who led us to tables under the trees. We all had the same, very good, set meal, during which there was a folk-dance representation of a country wedding. The Poles were also encouraged to join the dance, and after the jugs of wine we had all drunk, they needed little persuasion. At the end of the meal, having been told we could take our pottery wine mugs home, we once again boarded the coach and headed back into the city. A few of the Poles, hearing us chatting in English, began to sing the Beatles' 'Yellow submarine' and to call out names of English football teams. My brother, who knew the names of some Polish players, called them out, and this resulted in much enthusiastic cheering. Then one of the men took out a bottle of some clear spirits from his duffel-bag and insisted we all had a drink. Conversation was limited, but using Endre as interpreter, we were able to exchange a few words. We were first to get off the coach, and our departure heralded one or two cries of 'God save the Queen,' much laughing and much waving.

The following morning we decided to go to the castle area in Buda. We walked the medieval, cobbled streets and squares, visited the castle art gallery and museum, then made our way down the steep street which afforded glimpses of shady courtyards and numerous restaurants tucked in cellars, and was lined with small souvenir shops full of hand-embroidered blouses and cloths. The coloured tiles of the Matthias church's roof gleamed in the sun. Sitting on the turreted Fisherman's Bastion behind it were country people and Transylvanians selling more embroidery and lace. The panorama over the river to the whole of Pest on its far side, is compulsory viewing for all tourists. The afternoon we spent sitting on a large boat that took a lazy two hours to chug its way around the Margaret Island.

We had thought of going to a favourite restaurant that evening, called the Wine catacombs (*Borkatakomba*), on the edge of the city. It was a place that few of our friends knew, but all whom we had taken had liked it. We were just getting ready to leave when the doorbell rang. It was Feri, one of Paul's students from the Academy, who had come to see if he could borrow the score of a work he was to conduct but which was unavailable in the Budapest shops. We introduced him to Brian and suggested he might like to come with us to eat.

The bus journey took about forty minutes and we always found it difficult to know exactly where to get off since the entrance was via a car park at the foot of a hill, then through a large wooden door in the hillside itself. Standing in the doorway was a man in black trousers tucked into long black boots, a shirt with enormous wide embroidered sleeves, and a leather waistcoat. Smilingly, he led us into a dimly-lit tunnel that broadened out into a large cavern. It was noticeably cooler here under the ground, where the catacombs are still used for making and storing wine.

Lining both sides of one long 'tunnel' were huge empty wine barrels turned on their sides. Within each barrel was a wooden table and benches arranged around three sides, so that you actually sat inside the barrel. The barrel would quite comfortably have seated six people and we piled in and began to look at the menu. Each barrel had a coach lamp attached to the outside which, if switched on, signalled to the waiter. In the cavernous area at the far end were many more tables, and at the very end was a small stage where a gypsy band played and where there was folk-dancing.

We switched on our lamp and ordered *gulyás*. I had once made the mistake of cooking what was called 'Hungarian goulash', from an English recipe for Miklós on his first visit to us in England. Not telling him what it was, I gave him a good helping. 'Mmmm, this is good,' he said. I waited. 'What is it?' he asked. 'What do you think it is?' He considered the question very carefully. 'Irish stew?' he inquired.

Even Feri was forced to admit how good the restaurant *gulyás* was. Most Hungarians decry everything but their own mother's cooking.

'What are you doing tomorrow and Sunday?' asked Feri suddenly.

'Well, we don't know yet, it really depends on what Brian would like to see,' we replied.

'How about coming with me? I'm going home tomorrow, it's my mother's name-day, so there'll be lots of food.'

'Well... but how could you let them know, there's no time,' Paul said, knowing Feri's parents had no phone.

'That doesn't matter. I've told them all about you, they'll be really pleased to see you. Anyway,' he continued, noting our reservation, 'they're used to it. I'm always taking people home.'

The music had begun, and the switch which amplified the playing through a small speaker inside our barrel was broken in the 'on' position. We finished our soup and red wine, looking out of the end of the barrel every now and then to watch the dancing. No-one was hungry enough to eat a main dish, so we ordered pancakes, a heaped plateful with chopped walnuts and cream and covered with hot chocolate sauce, and some more wine.

'I'll pick you up at nine o'clock,' Feri said. 'It's about a two-hour drive.' He grimaced as the gypsy musicians began their journey around the tables and so, washing the remaining pancakes down with the last of the second bottle of Bull's Blood wine, we switched on our lamp to pay.

The following morning Feri was at the door before nine. 'I forgot to tell you yesterday,' he said, 'to take some warm clothes. It's much cooler up in the mountains.' We each packed a thick sweater, though we found it difficult to believe that the difference in temperature could possibly be so great.

Feri had parked in the square outside the Palm Cake Shop, giving Brian an excuse to nip in and buy one or two things for the trip. Meanwhile, I went to one of the flower stalls in the market and bought half a dozen gladioli.

'I didn't know you had a car,' observed Paul.

'I haven't,' replied Feri, 'it's a Trabant!' A comment we were to hear many times about this East German vehicle, the cheapest car available in Hungary. We clambered in. It was a tight squeeze, and Brian and I in the back had our knees almost under our chins. We spluttered off down the road, stopping soon after to buy petrol.

'This car has a very modern fuel gauge,' said Feri. We looked. 'Here,' he said, pointing to a blank space on the dashboard. 'When the car stops you know you've run out of petrol.'

In fact Trabant drivers had to keep a rough record of how much petrol they had put in and how far they had driven.

The engine was very noisy, like a motor-mower going at full throttle, and conversation was achieved only by sitting on the very edge of the back seat and yelling into Feri's and Paul's ears. 'You know, a horse once ate a part of a Trabant,' said Feri. 'They're made of fibreglass. I don't suppose you have them in England, do you?' We shook our heads. And yet this caricature of modern road travel cost 50,000 forints, and you had to wait about five years to get one. Feri told us the joke about the accident between an Englishman in his Jaguar, a West German in his BMW, and a Hungarian in his Trabant. All three cars were write-offs. 'I'll have to work a year before I can buy another Jaguar,' moaned the Englishman. 'And I'll have to work two years before I can buy another BMW,' continued the German. 'Huh! I'll have to work at least five years before I can buy another Trabant,' concluded the Hungarian, whereupon the other two looked at him and said, 'Well, why do you have to buy such an expensive car?' At the time Feri was speaking, the cost of a Trabant was one and a half times the average annual income.

We headed northwards in the direction of the Czechoslovakian border, climbing up into the Bükk mountains. The name of Feri's village was Bükkszenterzsébet, and every year on St. Elizabeth's day, the whole village joined in huge celebrations. Perhaps the most surprising feature of the villages we passed through were the number of imposing new houses being built. Feri laughed, 'Yes, everyone's building,' he said. 'These country people build their enormous houses with six rooms and two bathrooms and then you know what? They live just as they did in their little peasant houses, washing outside in a bowl of water, and living in the kitchen, not using the other rooms.'

We jolted our way off the main, and only made-up, road through the village, and up the dusty track to Feri's house. He jumped out of the car and opened the garden gate, then parked in the grassy drive with the single-storey house on one side, a small vineyard on the other.

Feri's father, in accordance with tradition also called Feri, and his mother, Mária, appeared at the same time – his father from the cellar where they kept their wine, his mother from the house. His young sister Mari, named after her mother, was also there. Their dog leapt about excitedly as Feri introduced us. Feri's father shook us all warmly by the hand and led us inside and into the small sitting-room. He opened a glass cabinet under the television set and took out a bottle of pálinka. Pálinka is a clear, fruit-flavoured spirit, potent and fiery, especially the home-made brew. It had, however, uses beyond its capacity for satisfying a desire for oblivion. Tamás had used it to weld his broken violin-bow resin, while during the previous winter's unavailability of antifreeze, drivers had used pálinka as an effective substitute. Filling six small glasses, he beamed at us all, 'May God give you a long life,' he said in traditional greeting. He knocked back the small glassful. I sipped mine, enjoying the slight burning sensation as it slithered down. We toasted both Márias' namedays and then sat down around the table.

Feri's father was a miner, a strong, ruddy-complexioned man who did shift-work on the coal-face. He quickly refilled empty glasses and laughed at our protests saying, 'It's good stuff, home-made.' Meanwhile, Feri's mother had disappeared into the kitchen. She was a large-boned, wide-hipped, heavy woman, with a warm motherly smile and a practical, unfussy manner.

'I'll just wash before we eat,' said Feri's father, leaving Feri to show us our rooms. After a brief look at the clarinet music his sister was learning, which was lying on the piano, Feri took us back out to the car to fetch our things. Outside, the sound of chickens and pigs was unmistakable and when I asked about them, Feri took us to where they were kept. There were two sties of pigs and several chicken runs. There were also a lot of rabbits which they did not eat, but sold to the Italians for their fur.

'Oh, by the way,' said Feri, 'the toilet is out here,' and pointed to a small wooden shed. When the door was opened, the smell hit us straight away. Inside was a large wooden box with a neatly carved hole in the centre to sit on, and a cesspit somewhere far underneath.

Taking our bags inside Feri showed us to our rooms, obviously kept in permanent readiness for guests. The enormous feather eiderdowns and pillows looked wonderfully inviting and all round the walls were family photos, souvenirs of past holidays, and a dresser full of precious Herend china. He took us past the kitchen to his parents' bedroom. On the far side was a curtain behind which was a bath and basin. 'You can wash here,' said Feri, 'and don't worry if no water comes out at first, we are not on the mains and the water has to be electrically pumped up from the well.'

Feri's mother called from the sitting room, extra chairs were brought and we all squeezed round the table. More pálinka was poured, and several bottles of wine stood ready on the piano. Then Feri's mother brought a large tureen of chicken and vegetable soup and a basket of fresh bread. The tureen, once emptied, was quickly refilled, as were our plates. It was followed by a platter of roast chicken and a variety of home-pickled vegetables. By now we felt quite replete, and I was wondering how on earth I would eat any of the cakes that were sure to follow.

We talked about Feri, and how he had come to be a musician. His grandmother had had a harmonium which he had taught himself to play at a young age. His parents, glad that at last he seemed to be interested in something other than reading, encouraged him to play. He soon began composing his own pieces and sent off to the main music shop in Budapest for scores, unbeknown to his parents, so when the postman arrived carrying heavy brown parcels, they were left to foot the bill. Later on they bought a piano for him and soon he was asking if he could go to a music school. There are countless music schools all over Hungary where children learn all the usual school subjects but where the emphasis is on music and everyone learns an instrument. As there was no such school in their small village, Feri had to travel every day to the town of Eger. He was given the choice of learning either the violin or the trumpet, his father categorically refused to put up with the sound of violin practice, so Feri became a trumpeter. A year or so later, he transferred to the Bartók conservatory in Budapest (for 14–18 year olds) and from there to the Liszt Academy.

While we had been chatting and drinking, the plate of chicken had been removed, but ominously, our dinner plates remained. A few minutes later another tureen was brought in, this time with stuffed cabbage. The leaves of the cabbage were filled with spicy minced meat and rice, eaten with a good dollop of sour cream. We could hardly move after eating as small a portion as was polite and then, of course, came the cakes...

Feri's mother, refusing all offers of help, cleared away the plates, while we sprawled in the worn armchairs and little Mari played one or two clarinet pieces. Two more plates of cakes were brought in and left on the table, and by seven o'clock the family was ready for supper: cold meat and cheese, salami, sausage, tomatoes, sweet yellow peppers, boiled eggs and bread and butter. More wine was fetched from the cellar together with a jug of fruit juice.

By nine o'clock Feri's parents were ready for bed they usually got up before five, due to the lack of mains water. They had no washing machine, and Feri's mother did all the washing by hand. Things were especially difficult after a long, dry spell, when it was sometimes necessary to fetch extra water from a stand pump, which is what many people in villages have to do. Apart from the obvious chores of shopping, cooking, cleaning and washing, there were the animals to be fed and looked after, the allotment in the neighbouring field to be tended, as well as the vineyard next to the house. And in addition there was the constant disruption to their lives caused by the regular changes in shift that Feri's father worked.

We were left together in the sitting room with an unopened wine bottle, but soon we too felt in need of sleep.

I still had to write something in a large guest book kept in the house, full of beautiful drawings and poems from those who had been to stay. Glancing through, I found entries from people of many nationalities, and I realised that what Feri had said was true: his parents were accustomed to his bringing friends home without warning.

Although it was dark, a last trip to the toilet was unavoidable. Some light from the house illuminated the drive, but beyond that lay total darkness. I fumbled my way past the chickens and towards the pigsties, to the little hut beside them. I opened the door and felt for the hole in the seat. By leaving the door slightly ajar I could vaguely see where I was and take a few breaths of fresh air at the same time. Through the gap I could see the outline of the vines standing in neat rows behind the fence, the fields stretching into the distance, and far beyond them, the Bükk mountains outlined against a darkening sky. I wondered what it must be like in the depths of winter looking out at a snow-blanketed landscape from this freezing hut. As I walked back past the vineyard I could hear the pigs grunting softly behind me, while ahead lay no light, no house, no sound.

The following morning, after a breakfast of cheese, eggs, toast and coffee – we declined the offer of an early-morning pálinka – we left Feri's Trabant and set off in his father's Lada for the caves at Aggtelek. The main street through the village was lined with people going to church, mostly elderly men in their best black Sunday boots and hats, top buttons of their shirts tightly fastened but without ties, and women in lace-up boots, dark coats and headscarves. The bells resounded down every street. There was a cool dampness in the air, a first hint of autumn that had been totally absent in Budapest, while a few wisps of mist hung over the fields.

The road wound through the forested hills, giving occasional glimpses of fields and valleys far below. There was hardly any traffic, just the occasional horse and cart or cyclist in the middle of the road. When we arrived at Aggtelek we were surprised to find only two other cars in the large car park under the trees. We all shivered as we got out of the car, but knowing it would be still colder underground, resisted the urge to put on our sweaters.

Ahead of us lay steep cliffs, and to the left a small museum and ticket office with one or two people in anoraks and rucksacks hanging about outside. The ground was wet and the trees dripped from the mist. A sign on the window of the ticket office announced that the next guided walk around the caves, which would last one hour, would leave in forty-five minutes, so we went into the museum. There was a display of rock samples, the history of the caves, and many photographs. Unfortunately, as in so many museums and places visited by tourists, all the captions were in Hungarian. We were the only people there though and so the curator was only too pleased to supply us with additional information.

A shout from outside indicated that the guide was ready to leave, so we bought our tickets and joined the half-dozen other people outside. Unfortunately, the end of August marked the end of the official tourist season at Aggtelek and the longer tours, which included a boat trip on an underground river in the caves, were no longer on offer. Aggtelek is a vast complex of caves which crosses the Hungarian-Czechoslovak border underground. All the caves were well lit, there are stalactites and stalagmites in a variety of colours, and many had been given names inspired by their shapes. A number of small underground streams had wooden bridges, and in other places duck-boards had been placed over the wettest areas. Leading from every cave were tunnels, some of them unlit, and we were warned more than once to keep together if we hoped to see daylight again. The most impressive cave was of immense proportions and was used for concerts. Rows of seats had been arranged and we sat while a tape was played through large speakers, the acoustics were perfect.

We emerged into sunshine and warmth, the mist having cleared. It was almost midday and everyone was hungry. On the far side of the car park was a sort of caravan we had not noticed when we had arrived, and it appeared to be selling food. It was selling pancakes, and a choice of fillings was printed on a list on the small window: walnut, poppyseed, cinnamon, curd cheese or cocoa. We bought two of each piled on to paper plates, taking also some serviettes and four glasses of strong, hot, black coffee.

We set off again, deciding to return by a different route, aiming to be home for a late lunch and return to Budapest in the early evening. According to the map we needed to take a minor road off to the right that would take us over the hill we were on, and back to the road to Bükkszenterzsébet. However, as we came to the turning we wanted, a road works sign and a trench right across the road blocked our path. There was nothing for it but to continue on the road we were on and hope that we could find another way home, although no other turning was shown on the map.

We were in luck. Some miles further along the road was a single-track lane leading off to the right, only there was a white barrier across it which we could not shift. But Feri spotted a small house almost hidden in the trees further up the track and walked towards it. We waited. After a few minutes he came strolling back accompanied by an elderly man carrying a large bunch of keys and a book as big as a telephone directory. He greeted us politely and explained that the road was in a nature reserve, not open to traffic, but if we would sign his book, declaring that we would drive at a maximum of 20 mph, not pick any flora or interfere with the fauna, picnic, or in any way damage anything, he would allow us through. Feri produced his driving licence and signed the book, and the man unlocked the barrier and waved us on.

We drove slowly, as birds flew shrieking up from the track, obviously unaccustomed to traffic. Weeds grew up in the middle of the lane, while bushes and trees brushed the sides of the car. Once a deer leaped into the undergrowth as we approached and rabbits scurried for their burrows. Then, quite unexpectedly, there would be a gap in the trees and we discovered just how high we were, seeing the steep rocks and the sparse grass and wild flowers in the crags, and the clouds floating past below us casting shadows across the valley. This was a completely different landscape from the one we had left behind on the road below. It was wild, totally unpopulated. The road was short, leading over the hill and down the other side, and where it rejoined the main road there was a 'No-entry' sign, and another barrier which was, however, not locked.

Driving back into Bükkszenterzsébet, most people had already eaten and many were busy on the fields in the warm sun. Whole families were bent double, hoeing and weeding, the women in bright headscarves   colourful blobs on the brown landscape. Their bicycles were lying between the grass verge and the edge of the field together with bags containing food and drink.

Back at Feri's home, pálinka glasses stood ready on the table, though not for Feri who still had to drive, nor for his father who was soon leaving to work a night-shift. Lunch was soup, stuffed peppers, roast pork and finally coffee and cake. Feri had a choir rehearsal in Budapest that evening, so we slowly gathered up our things and put them in the car. One final trip to the loo and we were ready to leave. At the last moment, Feri's mother appeared with small packets of food wrapped in silver foil, eggs, cakes and cold meat for Feri, so he should not starve before his next visit, and bottles of home-made pálinka and wine for us. Feri's parents and sister stood at the gate waving and calling to us all to come again soon as we spluttered our way down to the main road, followed by an excitedly barking dog.

★ ★ ★ ★ ★

September was drawing to a close, my brother's visit was over, and Paul and I returned to our usual daily routine. The hot weather continued beyond when the clocks were put back and into October – a real Indian summer.

I soon received a postcard, in reply to my own, from Virginia in Dabas. She suggested we go and visit them the following weekend. Thus, we caught the train from the terminus of the metro line and on arrival at the small, country station, scoured the crowd for someone carrying a carrier bag bearing the American flag. We soon spotted Virginia, with her dark, curly hair and welcoming smile. She led us to a Trabant parked outside the station building, saying how much she had been looking forward to seeing us.

We drove past the church where her husband, Joseph, was the minister and on to the next corner where their house stood. It was an old, rambling vicarage with crumbling plaster walls, standing on a huge plot of land. Many trees surrounded it, and the verandah leading to the paint-flaked front door was covered with ivy and grapevines.

We followed Virginia into the large, but dark kitchen where she made tea which we carried out to the heavy, wooden table on the verandah, and seated in the shade of the ripening grapes and dusty ivy, she told us how she had come to Hungary. 'And now I'm studying theology at the Lutheran College in Budapest,' she concluded.

'What, in Hungarian?' I asked incredulously.

'Yes. I take a cassette-recorder to tape the lectures, and then I write them down at home and look up all the things I can't understand.'

We could hardly find words to express our admiration. 'Are you having Hungarian lessons?' asked Paul.

'Yes,' she replied. 'I went to Ócsa, the town between here and Budapest, and went to the local grammar school. I found the English teacher there, called Eta, and we made an agreement that I would give her practice and help with her English if she would teach me Hungarian. We meet once or twice a week.'

Joseph arrived home, a tall, handsome man who welcomed us warmly in good English. Having repeated to him the gist of our story as to how we came to be in Hungary, Virginià and I walked down the steps from the terrace and to a small area of the garden where she was growing vegetables. 'Where is the end of your plot of land?' I asked, surveying the large area of grass and trees.

'See where that ruined outbuilding is?' she said, pointing to a small dilapidated, stone structure. 'That marks the boundary. And guess what? Someone lives in there. He was an aristocrat, he had all his property confiscated and then he became an alcoholic. We don't really know his whole history, but he's homeless and lives in there   of course there's no heating or anything.' Seeing my surprise she continued, 'And see that huge house over there?' I followed her gaze. 'The local party secretary lives there, of course they won't even speak to us.'

We spent the remainder of the afternoon soaking up the last mellow rays of sun as they filtered through the vine leaves, exchanging tales of our Hungarian experiences, and when the shadows lengthened we prepared to leave for the station. As Virginia started the engine of the Trabant an elderly woman rode up on a black, squeaky bicycle and asked where she might find Joseph. 'People come and go all day long,' Virginia observed. 'Without a telephone everyone has to come personally whether they want to arrange a funeral or they just need a key to the church. If you're trying to work it can be really irritating, however kind and friendly the people here are,' she said. We squeezed into the car and bumped off down the unmade road in a cloud of dust, agreeing to keep in touch and meet again soon in Budapest.

★ ★ ★ ★ ★

I had brought my cello back with me from England that summer with the intention of restarting lessons (I had had four months' tuition in England), in all probability with one of Paul's students. Thus it was that, on the last Sunday in

September, I met Zoli. He was 21, had quite a good passive knowledge of English and was an extremely talented cellist. He came literally skipping up the stairs at Garay Square to start teaching me. It was only that morning that I had taken the instrument out of its case, and found that the fingerboard, which had been slightly loose in England, had actually parted company from the rest of the cello. Luckily, Zoli had brought his own instrument with him. He looked surprised when I suggested I play on it, but then agreed, and asked me to play a scale. After playing just a few notes, Zoli stopped me. 'What do you think of how it sounds?' he asked me. I began to try and excuse myself, saying I had not played for a year and that anyway I was a beginner and my teacher in England, a member of a leading British Symphony Orchestra, had said I could hardly expect to make a good tone so early on. Zoli did not comment. Then, 'What about your thumbs don't they hurt you?' he asked. I was amazed. My thumbs were not hurting then, after only a minute of playing, but they definitely had hurt in England after about twenty minutes' practice. When I had asked my teacher about it she had simply told me that I was using my muscles in a different way from when I played the piano, that I should not practise too much and I would get used to it.

'How do you know?' I asked Zoli.

'I can see from the way you hold the cello and especially how you hold the bow,' he replied.

We decided that I should begin again from the beginning, and the remainder of the lesson took place in the bathroom much to the amusement of Paul who, returning from shopping, found us both bent over the half-filled bath dragging a face-cloth up and down on the surface of the water. My 'homework' was to consist of this daily exercise, plus others such as picking up salt cellars off the table, or holding the top of the back of a chair and swinging it towards me on its two back legs, always checking that my thumb muscle was soft and relaxed – 'loosey' as Zoli said.

At the end of the two-hour lesson I asked Zoli what I owed him. He looked offended. He said that when Paul asked him if he would teach me he had decided it would be good for him, and so he wanted no payment. As we walked towards the door I tried to stuff a 100-forint note into his pocket. For a moment he looked hurt then, hoisting his cello onto his shoulder, he dropped the money on a chair and ran down the steps two at a time, waving and smiling as he went. Thereafter it was a weekly battle to get him to take any payment.

At the end of October I had agreed to teach at one of Lingua's country courses, this time at a glass factory in Salgótarján, a town in the north, close to the Czechoslovak border. It meant going on a Sunday and returning the following Saturday afternoon. I decided to drive, since the flat I was to stay in was at the opposite end of the town from where I was to teach, and I would otherwise have to catch two buses each way. I made a last trip over to Lingua to collect the books, cassettes and other materials I would need and then, taking heed of Miklós's advice and my experience of the weather in the Bükk at Feri's, I packed some warm clothes and finally my cello bow – I was now at last permitted to pick it up though not to use it on the cello.

I left on the Sunday afternoon and it was already dusk as I passed the town of Hatvan, its name 'Sixty' indicating its distance from Budapest. Many towns and villages have quaint or funny names when translated, for example the villages of Sári (Sarah) and Bugyi (knickers). (Hence the old joke that to get to Sarah you have to go through knickers!)

The two-lane motorway was dimly lit, had no cats' eyes, inadequate road signs, and the frequent road works were so badly illuminated and sign-posted that I did not wonder at the many road accidents that occurred. At the permitted maximum speed of 60 mph and with the poor lighting, it was all but impossible to react to the obstacle course of lane changes. However, driving through the smaller villages which have no street lighting at all was far worse, with a preponderance of peasant cyclists in black clothes and no lights swerving from one side of the road to the other, in states varying from the mildly tipsy to the totally paralytic.

Salgótarján was in a long valley, a town of one steel and two glass factories with its inhabitants housed for the most part in prefabricated concrete blocks of flats. Its one redeeming feature is the wooded hills that lie between it and the Czechoslovak border, but in late October the trees were already bare and so my impression remained unfavourable. The students were friendly but rather distant in comparison with those I had taught in Baja and Orosháza, not only with me, but with each other. The canteen food, a highlight at the sister glass factory in Orosháza, was here practically inedible, especially the honey-sweet tomato soup. I was shown round the factory which was of course interesting, and it made me curious to know if factory workers in England also had to work in such searing temperatures, dust and noise. I was given a small box containing five breathalyser tubes from one of the students who regularly had to use them to monitor workers dealing with machines and subsequently to send them home if the result showed positive.

It was a quiet week in this quiet town and I created a stir as I drove through the centre at 7.30 am – certainly few tourists go to Salgótarján, particularly in a right-hand drive car where the driver seems to be absent to anyone giving no more than a cursory glance. A policeman, substituting for broken traffic lights at one junction, stopped waving his arms about to stare open-mouthed as I went past. The great gossip of the time was a story concerning a group of housewives who had set up a brothel in the home of one of their number which had just been uncovered by the police. Otherwise life consisted of shift-work at the factory and family life in concrete blocks, and an occasional trip to the one cinema or the concrete shopping centre. It would be untrue to say that I was not glad to leave and head back to Budapest on a sunny, frosty

Saturday lunchtime, leaving Salgótarján a receding image in my rear-view mirror.

Back in Budapest I felt that winter had almost arrived. Standing waiting for my No. 67 tram at Keleti station I watched as the many stone blocks in the pedestrian area below road level were cleared away   blocks on which students and travellers had sat in the sun, peasants from the country waiting for trains home on summer afternoons or tired men drinking beer in the early evening after work. Coach loads of tourists had dwindled to all but a few from Poland in the car park behind the station, and the black leather coat brigade was once again becoming evident.

★ ★ ★ ★ ★

As November progressed our thoughts turned once again to Christmas and the train journey to Germany. This time visas and tickets were procured without difficulty. Buying presents was time-consuming but enjoyable, especially from the small street stalls, and it was while wandering along the boulevard towards Margaret Bridge that I suddenly found myself in Fürst Sándor Street. A slight feeling of panic seized me as memories flooded back from five years before.

It was in 1978 that our whole relationship with Hungary had begun. In writing both his Ph.D. and a book on the composer Liszt, Paul had applied for and received a two-month British Council scholarship to work in Budapest.

We travelled together to Victoria Station on January 31st and Paul began the 24-hour journey to Budapest. He was met at Keleti station by Miklós who took Paul first to the police station to register him, and then on to the accommodation that had been arranged for him in a flat in Fürst Sándor Street. The flat belonged to a fifty-year-old divorcee, Mrs H., whose son was at university. The flat was quite large and comfortably furnished with antiques and oil paintings.

Mrs H. spoke no English so when Miklós was not there to interpret, communication between herself and Paul was limited to their mutual knowledge of basic German. On arriving, she asked Paul, through Miklós, if he wanted her to provide him with breakfast and an evening meal. He agreed and asked how much it would cost, his accommodation already having been paid for by the Hungarian equivalent of the British Council. She dismissed the question out of hand and Miklós suggested to Paul that he buy her some presents at the end of his stay since she was refusing money. Then, after writing down enough Hungarian words to enable Paul to buy an airmail letter from the tobacconist next door, and arranging to come at 8 am the following morning, Miklós left.

Although employed to interpret for only three days, Miklós and Paul became firm friends and met almost daily. Miklós began to teach Paul the rudiments of Hungarian while Paul gave Miklós the then rare opportunity of conversing with a native English speaker. Occasionally Miklós would give Paul a Hungarian lesson at the flat, but Paul soon realised that, for some reason, this appeared to trouble Mrs H. 'Has Miklós been here again?' she would ask upon her return from work, looking at the cigarette stubs in the ashtray. It was obvious that she did not like him, nor did she approve of Paul's continuing friendship with him.

I was to visit Budapest for the last two weeks of Paul's stay and we would return to England together. Paul approached Mrs H. with the idea and asked if I could bring some things for her from England since she would not accept payment for our food. So I received a list: jeans and a denim jacket for her son, a skirt and blouse for her, whisky, cassettes and various other items.

I staggered through the customs with my two heavy cases. I was stopped. 'Please open your cases.' I did. The customs officer held up the new jeans. 'Are these presents for somebody? And what about the whisky and these cassettes?'

Something warned me not to tell the truth. 'They're for my husband, he's been here for two months, he's studying here,' I replied. Luckily there were no more questions.

Mrs H. was delighted with the presents, and the clothes fitted. My two weeks with Paul passed in visiting museums, going to concerts, and a memorable trip to the cathedral in Esztergom, the day when winter's snows melted in an upsurge of sixteen degrees of spring sunshine.

Once or twice we met Miklós and went out for a meal. We were both amazed at the cheapness and quality both of restaurants and supermarket food. We bought large numbers of classical records, books and sheet music and had practically no money left the day before we were to leave.

That morning, a Friday, we awoke with no other plan than going to Miklós's and Rézi's flat for a meal in the evening. Mrs H. had already left for work at seven o'clock as usual, but had left a note in the kitchen beside our breakfast. It looked like a bill: itemised were eight weeks' food for Paul and two weeks' for myself. The total far exceeded any realistic calculation of what two weeks' food could have cost, even if we had eaten in restaurants for the entire duration. Nowhere were the purchases from England mentioned. A further large sum had been added for telephone calls we had simply not made. We rang Miklós who soon came round and rang Mrs H. at work. He began trying to explain the absurdity of her demands but she hung up. It was then we learnt that their antipathy to one another was mutual. Miklós told us not to worry, but to bring the 'bill' with us that evening.

Miklós and Rézi lived with her parents in a leafy area of Buda. Rézi had cooked a wonderful meal and they gave us a beautifully illustrated book on the history of Hungary as a parting present. Finally, Miklós wrote a note for us by way of reply to what Mrs H. had left us, telling her she should be more than satisfied with the things I had brought since, even if she had been able to buy them in Hungary, they would have cost several times the amount on her bill.

Mrs H. was asleep when we returned, so we left the note in the kitchen and went to bed. At six o'clock the following morning our door was flung open and Mrs H. stormed into the room. She was screaming and brandishing the note above her head. In the heat of the moment she abandoned all but her native Hungarian, but the cause of her hysteria was not difficult to guess. Two doors led into our bedroom and she continued to run in through one and out of the other, screaming all the time. Then suddenly, something caught her eye and she made a lunge for the table in our room. It was my keys. She obviously had thoughts of locking us in the flat. I jumped out of bed and snatched the keys before she could reach them. She ran from our room and began to make a telephone call.

We got dressed quickly and packed the last of our belongings but had no idea what to do next. I looked carefully through the open door into the sitting room. She was not there. We decided to risk a call to Miklós. 'Miklós? Thank God. She's gone mad about your note. She tried to take away our keys. Can't you try and talk to her?' 'I'll try, but I'm not optimistic,' came the reply.

Mrs H. reappeared. I handed the receiver to her. She said a few words and then handed the phone back. 'It's no good,' Miklós told us, 'she won't discuss it at all. I'll go to the office which rented the room for you and try to sort things out.'

Mrs H. approached us again with a copy of the bill she had given us, pointing to the total sum of money she wanted us to pay her. I asked in German, 'And what about what I brought you?' She walked off back to the phone and we adjourned to the kitchen for some breakfast.

Some time and many phone calls later, she came to the kitchen with her bill and started shouting again, threatening to call the police if we did not pay. I told her we had no money left and I would have to ring the embassy to find out which bank was open on a Saturday. It was a bluff, I had no intention of trying to get to a bank, I merely wanted to ask someone what the best course of action was in the circumstances. She allowed me to ring. 'Hallo, British Embassy?' I enquired.

'Yes.'

I outlined our predicament as briefly as I could.

'I'm sorry, madam,' came the smooth reply as I finished, 'We're closed on Saturdays.'

'But you can't be closed!' I shouted. 'We're likely to be arrested!'

'Just a minute...' I waited.

The voice returned. 'We recommend you leave the building as quickly as possible and go to the airport and wait for your plane.'

I thanked him and hung up.

'Let's pretend we're going to the bank and make a run for it,' Paul suggested. We told Mrs H. that we would go to the bank at nine, so a truce ensued during which we carried our cases into the hall and she, still in her nightdress, continued to make phone calls.

We waited until she seemed sufficiently deep in conversation for us to risk making a bolt for it. The hitch was that we were on the fifth floor and the lift was not working. We ran out, cases in hand, to hear a shriek of horror behind us and shouts of '*Rendőrség! Rendőrség!* (Police! Police!).

It was not easy to carry the heavily laden cases down the stairs at any speed. Mrs H. soon caught up with us and tried to tear my handbag off my shoulder, realising that to take away our tickets and passports would pre-empt our escape. Having failed in this, she grabbed my suitcase and we wrestled with it until the handle came off and I continued my descent kicking the suitcase ahead of me. By this time, anyone in the building who had not gone to work was standing in their doorway watching in silent disbelief. Paul was waiting for me on the second floor, but as I reached him, a flat door behind him opened and hands half-beckoned, half-pulled us in. The door was quickly closed behind us.

'What's wrong?' asked an elderly woman in perfect English, taking us into the sitting room. We explained the whole story. She was kind, though I felt she did not quite believe it all. 'How terrible,' she said. 'Your first visit to Hungary and you will never want to come back. But how can I help you? Shall I call a taxi for you?' We consented gratefully.

Meanwhile, Mrs H. banged on the front door and shouted in an affected gruff voice, 'This is the police!' It was bizarre.

The taxi arrived in the street below, but we had no idea how to get past Mrs H. In the event we found her sitting, still in nightdress and dressing-gown, on the stairs outside. She followed us meekly out into the street, but as we got into the taxi she once again produced her bill and indicated that she wanted Paul's signature on it as an acknowledgement that he owed the money. He wrote a capital P. and M. followed by a scribble. She scoffed, and showed it to the bemused taxi driver asking, 'That's not a signature, is it?' He shrugged and revved his engine. 'I'm going to the office to check your signature, and if it's no good I'm coming after you to the airport,' she threatened as she allowed the taxi to leave.

When we were back in England Miklós rang to say that Mrs H. had been to the office and complained that Paul hit her, but that they had believed his and our story, and would never again billet anyone with her.

And now here I stood once more, practically outside her front door. I wondered if we would recognise one another if we did meet, and what her reaction might be. I did not wait to find out.

★ ★ ★ ★ ★

Christmas came and went, and 1984 began with a week spent in Orosháza. Lingua was doing well with an abundance of new courses and new students. They had expanded into two more rooms on the same floor of the building and bought a lot of new equipment.

Orosháza was my favourite country course. Lessons were held and teachers accommodated at the glass factory's guesthouse on a lakeside. It was a large, single-storey building, predominantly of windows, with long lawns sloping down to the water's edge. Each day's lessons ended with some kind of party or an evening spent at the home of one of the students. There was also a favourite café we would frequent though the friendly waitress Ibolya (Violet) has probably never forgotten the day Paul called her *uborka* (cucumber) by mistake.

Through us they learnt to love both a language and its culture, and with them we formed special friendships that lasted many years beyond the lessons. One memorable Saturday separating the two weeks of a course, we decided we would all go to the champagne-bottling plant at Kecskemét whose bottles were made in Orosháza. János, Miklós and Paul were all there so, with about a dozen students we set off in convoy for Kecskemét. We were met by our students' counterparts and taken for champagne tasting. Six long, slim glasses containing different varieties of champagne were poured for each of us. After three glasses I, for one, had ceased to notice anything but the increasing effect, the taste fast becoming of secondary consideration. We were then presented with a bottle of the one we liked best and led down into a cool, dark cellar furnished with long wooden tables laden with cold food. My memory of events became hazy from that point on, and it was only late Sunday morning that I found out whose car I had come back in, and that I had slept throughout the journey.

The succeeding months' work was all in Budapest, and I resumed regular cello lessons and teaching. With no telephone here either, our evenings were unpredictable. We could be alone at six and then with several friends by seven, since communication necessitated seeing one another personally, and anyone could call in at any time.

It was in February 1984, after eighteen months, that we met our first English person living in Budapest. Caroline had in fact come to Hungary in 1967, married her pen-friend, a painter, had three sons and was now living in a village on the city boundary. She was able to tell us of about half a dozen other British people also resident in Budapest, all of whom had married Hungarians. We had thus far deliberately not sought out English people, not wanting to be drawn into some kind of expatriates' circle, but none in fact existed. Caroline was a fount of information on any subject we touched upon, and a week later she left a message in our letterbox asking if we would like to do a voice recording at a film studio with her.

It was the first time I had undertaken such work and my first task was for a film about teaching very young children the Kodály method of singing. Later recordings varied from language-teaching cassettes (English-made cassettes being unavailable), and voice-overs for documentary films about Hungary. The translation of the original Hungarian text was poor and the first hour had to be spent correcting it, the many scribbled alterations rendering the text all but illegible so that we made many errors in our reading. But it was a new experience, and many similar ones were to follow, always in a relaxed atmosphere of patient technicians and long coffee breaks necessitated by faulty equipment or missing pages of script.

May 1st was sunny, and because I had missed the previous May Day celebrations, I was determined to go. The scale of the event was unmatched by anything else in the year. For weeks before, a loudspeaker system was set up along the entire length of Dózsa György Street and in the City Park. Red banners proclaimed the Hungarians' thanks to their brothers in the Soviet Union and the ever-strengthening crusade towards Communism. It was a fineable offence not to hang the Hungarian and Red flags outside every building in the country.

In every factory and office block employees were 'volunteered' to march as representatives of their place of work. On the day itself groups of people would begin to gather in every side street off Dózsa György Street as early as six a.m, banners, balloons and beer in hand. Their numbers swelled to tens of thousands by ten a.m., the official start of the procession. Then the tribune next to the statue of Lenin would fill with the leaders of the Party, and socialist workers' songs would boom out through every speaker.

On the live television broadcast, a homogeneous mass of banner-waving people could be seen singing as they marched the length of Dózsa György Street for two hours or so, while the voice over the speakers called, 'Long live the Red Star shoe factory of...; Long live the Socialist Brotherhood Co-operative farm of...'. I walked out of the house into Garay Square and was swept along with the crowd. It would have been impossible either to stop or turn back. I found myself marching with the Union of Shipworkers. Many had brought their children, hoisted up on their shoulders, waving balloons. I looked around me. No-one was singing. All the cheering, all the singing, was coming from the gray speakers on every tree and lamp-post. The marchers were struggling against the noise to carry on conversations with husband, wife, child or friend. 'Pisti, pass me the beer!' shouted one, and a bottle was duly passed, swigged from and returned. 'Where are we meeting Ági and Éva?' a woman shouted. 'By the fountain in the park   they've got the food,' came her friend's reply. As we passed the tribune few cast more than a glance at their leaders, they just walked past as they might have done to a football match, smoking, chatting, glad to have a day off work and to be out in the sunshine. Free beer was provided in the park near Heroes' Square, where groups of friends and colleagues sprawled on the grass, and many fell asleep from the combined effects of sunshine and alcohol.

★ ★ ★ ★ ★

It must have been some time towards the end of June that Rózsi néni came to collect the rent, saying that Zoli bácsi was still ill. Her daughter and family were again expected in

August and we told her we would also be travelling to England and returning at the beginning of September. It was in fact a relief to escape from the relentless sunshine and temperatures well into the 30s.

We completed the usual round of visits to family and friends, including Sue and Steve with their new baby. The first two weeks were a blissful rest from the endless stream of exhausting challenges which constituted everyday life in Budapest. But then came the restlessness we had experienced the previous year, and we started to count the days until our return.

A few days after arriving back in Budapest, Rózsi néni appeared.

'How's Zoli bácsi?' we asked.

'No better,' she said, shaking her head. We invited her to sit down, gave her the rent and offered her some tea. 'My daughter's coming back from Canada,' she suddenly announced. 'She didn't pass her exams in medicine and she doesn't want to stay there if she can't work.'

We were amazed, after all that Endre had told us. 'When are they coming back?' I asked. 'By Christmas. But they don't want to live here in Garay Square,' she continued. 'They want me to find them a new flat.' She had stood up and was making her way towards the front door. 'You like it here though, don't you?' she said, looking around. We nodded. 'This flat's been in the family for a long time. Oh well, after Canada I suppose...' she tailed off, opening the door.

We were stunned. For us, this would be the worst time to move, just when term was starting. We would hardly have time to go flat-hunting. And we had no idea how much time we would have if the flat had to be swapped before Christmas. When we told Endre, he maintained that there was absolutely no chance of Anna and her family returning from Canada. What he could imagine was that the husband's permit was not going to be extended by the Hungarian state, and that they were now in the position of having to return or stay in Canada illegally, in other words, defect. If they chose to stay, the Garay Square flat, which was in Anna's name, but was of course a state flat, would automatically be confiscated. The only way to preclude this would be to swap the flat, not with another state flat, but with a privately-owned flat. A private flat was worth twice as much as a state one, so that someone wanting to live in a much larger flat could swap their small private one with someone who had a large state one. Endre concluded that this was what was happening. Rózsi néni would find a small private flat and swap it for Garay Square. Having done this she could quite legally sell the new flat and thus nothing would be lost if her daughter decided to stay in Canada. If however, the authorities suspected what was going on, they would intervene.

September passed with no new developments, but at the beginning of October Rózsi néni called again.

'How is Zoli bácsi?' we enquired.

'No better,' she sighed. 'I really came to tell you that I have advertised the flat and one or two people want to come and see it.' She paused. 'What are you going to do? Are you going back to England?'

'Oh no,' we replied. 'We'll find another place to rent,' we said, more optimistically than we felt.

Rózsi néni did bring some people to look at the flat but we heard nothing of whether they wanted to buy it. However, we had already begun to tell all our friends, acquaintances and students that we were looking for a new place to rent.

One day, still in October, I had just come home from teaching early in the afternoon when there was a knock at the door. Standing outside were two men in suits, one of whom looked vaguely familiar. They produced police IDs and asked if they could come in. Only one spoke, the other just looked on. Casually they walked along the hall towards the sitting room.

'I'm from KEOKH,' said the man whose face I thought I knew.

'Yes, I remember,' I replied.

'How long have you been here now?' he asked, again in a casual manner.

I wondered what on earth this was all about, what we could possibly have done to warrant a visit and where the conversation might be leading.

'Do you mean in Hungary?'

He nodded. He knew the answer of course, every detail of our stay was documented in KEOKH.

'Two years,' I replied.

'And how long have you been here in Garay Square?'

'Just over a year,' I said.

'May I look into the other rooms?' he asked. 'We always like to see that foreigners are suitably accommodated,' he added by way of explanation. I led the way, both men following into the two small bedrooms leading off the sitting-room. 'Are you satisfied with the flat?' he asked.

'Yes, of course.'

'Who is renting it to you?'

I told him.

Everything seemed to be falling into place. He paused. 'Well, thank you, I think we'll be going now,' he said as they headed back along the hall. 'Goodbye,' said one, while the other merely nodded his farewell.

'Goodbye,' I said, closing the door, feeling unsettled. I could hardly imagine that our living conditions were of any interest whatsoever to the police, and if they were, then why had they come only now after two years? No. Endre must have guessed correctly, and somehow the police had already become aware of Rózsi néni's scheme.

Yet if we felt that we were objects of suspicion to the Hungarian police we knew we were no less so to the English. Not long before, Paul had been to the British Council Library in the embassy. Arriving early, he waited outside the library door. As he stood alone in silence, alongside the empty coat rails in the cloakroom, he heard a voice on the other side of the door. 'Yes, I wonder what these Merricks are *really* doing here.'

Early in November János told us of a flat we would probably be able to rent, on the second floor of a house in Szinyei Merse Street. It belonged to József, a colleague of János's wife who worked at UNESCO, and János arranged a time for us to meet József at the flat a week later.

At about the same time, we had a visit from a woman we had never seen before. She called one morning and introduced herself as the local leader of the Communist Party. She said she had come to collect Zoli bácsi's party membership book as he had recently died. We had heard nothing of this, and told her that we had no idea where the book might be. We gave her Rózsi néni's telephone number and she left. That same afternoon, Rózsi néni arrived with her sister to collect the rent. Not quite knowing what to say with regard to Zoli bácsi, we decided to feign ignorance.

'How is Zoli bácsi?' we asked.

'No better,' came the astounding reply.

We did not pursue the subject, but later asked our neighbour Manci néni. 'Oh yes, he died about a week ago,' she told us. 'I saw it in the paper.'

A few days later we went to see the flat in Szinyei Street. The building was quite the worst in the narrow run-down street. Its graying pink plaster was falling off in chunks, and its stonework was scarred with countless bullet marks from the 1944-45 siege, and 1956. Unlike either the Dózsa György building or Garay Square, this had no pretensions to grandeur. The courtyard was an unrelieved area of concrete, empty but for a large iron stand on which carpets could be beaten. A strange, black wheelchair type of contraption was parked outside one of the ground floor doors near the customary black bins and letterboxes.

We walked up the narrow, winding staircase from the courtyard to the second floor. The walkway was equally narrow and we found that József's flat was in the very far corner. We knocked on the small, brown door and József ushered us into a tiny dark hall, and then into a slightly less dark area containing a desk and a small cupboard. Leading off this was the room, which was light and cheerful and had a beautiful wooden gallery. Wooden steps led up to a large platform on which one could sleep and store things, while underneath was a sofa, bookshelves and another desk. The room contained little other furniture. Leading directly off it came in turn the small kitchen and recently modernised bathroom.

József explained that it was his wife's flat but that they had moved out of Budapest to a village just outside the city boundary. He hated the noise and pollution of city life. He wanted 4,500 forints a month for the rent, which considering the size and condition of the place in comparison with Garay Square's 5,000 forints, seemed rather high. But winter was approaching, and although no flat swap seemed imminent, we wanted to complete the move before the first snow. Endre had tried to persuade us to stay at Garay Square, but it seemed that even if Rózsi néni could not carry out her plan, and even if Anna did not return from Canada, the council would take away the flat and we would have to leave anyway.

We agreed with József that I should collect the key from him in the last days of November, and that we would move in on December 1st. On our way home we decided to tell Rózsi néni that we were moving on December 8th to avoid the sort of supervision with moving out that we had endured with our moving in. Friends were asked to help, and two students I had been teaching privately for a year volunteered both their own help and that of a friend who owned a jeep. Meanwhile, we brought up our old English boxes from the cellar and began the arduous task of packing.

Towards the end of the month I rang József at work and we arranged to meet at Szinyei Street. When I arrived he was already there. 'Come in,' he said, taking me into the main room. 'Sit down. I'm afraid there's a bit of a problem.' I waited. 'It seems that my wife and I are going to be divorced, and she wants to come and live here.'

I was aghast. 'But why didn't you tell us anything before?' I asked. 'We've nearly finished packing and we've told our landlady we're moving out in a couple of weeks, and we haven't got anywhere else to go!'

'Don't worry,' said József, 'she couldn't possibly live alone with the children; she's never lived alone. This all happened once before and she didn't last the month here. And this flat is totally unsuitable for children, much too small.'

'Well, what's going to happen then?' I asked.

'I've already given her an ultimatum. Either she moves out by the end of the week, or she stops threatening to. If you ring me on Friday at work I'll let you know, but I'm quite certain she won't leave,' he said.

Feeling totally depressed and helpless I started out for home. I could not believe that the situation could have developed so dramatically since our last meeting. I told the news to Paul, who was equally shocked. We sat and looked at the sea of half-packed boxes all around us and wondered whether to continue packing or start unpacking. We did neither until Friday when I rang József and he said we could go ahead, his wife was not moving out.

By the evening of November 30th the red, flagstone floor of the hall was lined with boxes, and the black heavy furniture had been moved back into position in the sitting-room. The Garay Square flat resumed its original atmosphere of silent anticipation of a return of several generations of now deceased occupiers. We removed our names from the post box and the front door. Then, from the once again uncurtained window, we watched for the last time as the cat woman shuffled away from the gates of the silent market.

Courtyard and Characters
SZINYEI MERSE PÁL STREET

It was sunny but frosty as we dragged our boxes out into the street. János had arrived early but Miklós was in the country teaching. My students Ági and Kazi came soon afterwards with their friend István in his jeep. I had begun to teach Ági and Kazi when we moved to Garay Square. Ági taught at the College of Foreign Trade while Kazi worked for a state trading company. Both were always well dressed and reflected attitudes far more 'western' than other Hungarians we knew. We had bought the two floral armchairs from Rózsi néni together with an old table, the straw-upholstered chairs and the cheese plant, and I now sat in one of the armchairs out on the pavement. I felt slightly nervous that Rózsi néni might have got to know that we were moving and would turn up unexpectedly.

Imre was already busy in his workshop. He put his head out around the door. 'Moving?' he asked.

'Yes, she's swapping the flat,' I answered. He nodded.

'Up you get!' interrupted István, 'We'll take the furniture first and come back for the boxes.' He took Paul with him and I wandered back upstairs leaving Ági to watch the things on the pavement.

We already had everything outside by the time István and Paul returned. One more trip to and from Szinyei and we were ready to load the last things into the jeep. Ági left to go home while János, Kazi and I took the trolley bus to our new flat leaving István and Paul to go ahead.

It had been no easy task to manoeuvre the furniture up the spiral staircase or along the walkway. Gradually we carried up the boxes, panting clouds of moist warmth into the bitingly cold December air, our arms aching. István was limping badly and I learnt from Paul that he had twisted his leg on the way upstairs while carrying one of the armchairs.

Kazi caught my glum look as I gazed at the crumbling walls, the other flat doors around the walkway and the concrete courtyard below, our only view from the window. 'You'll see, it'll be fine. It isn't a bad flat and this is a better area than Garay Square.' He subscribed to Endre's view that the Garay Square area should be demolished. He and Ági lived in a huge flat opposite the botanical gardens on Dózsa György Street, a mere five minutes' walk away from Szinyei. He had taken over the flat from his widowed father who had remarried and moved into his new wife's home. The flat was furnished with antiques and had an atmosphere of decayed elegance.

Kazi and István left, and Paul, János and I decided to go out and eat. It was already dark at four o'clock and we had no energy left to start unpacking more than our bedding. We had bought two foam mattresses which just fitted on the gallery, and after I had put a few plants alongside, the room seemed homely and inviting.

The following day we got up late and had just started unpacking when there was a knock on the front door – it had no doorbell. I was greeted by a woman of about sixty: 'I'm your neighbour, Mrs. Varga', she said. 'If we can help in any way just come over. Mrs. Nagy over there has a phone, she's the only person with one – we all use it,' she said, pointing to the door on the opposite side of the courtyard on our floor. 'Is your heating working alright?' she asked.

'Fine, thank you.' I replied.

'Good, well I'll let you carry on unpacking then,' and with a cheery smile she went back into her flat.

Four days later we had the first heavy fall of snow. We had moved just in time once again. We had planned to travel on the Meridian train to Germany for Christmas, though this time I would return alone while Paul went on to England to take his Ph.D. viva on Liszt.

It was in these last days before we left that Paul met an English composition student at the Music Academy. Laurence was twenty-one, his parents had left Hungary at the time of the '56 revolution and gone to England where he was born. One evening Paul brought Laurence home for a meal and we all got on marvellously. He was witty, entertaining and we found we shared common tastes in music.

Laurence could not afford to travel home for Christmas but what bothered him more was that there had been no hot water in his flat for the past few weeks. The flats in the building had been sold to their tenants by the council, but the central boiler which provided hot water to all the flats had since broken down completely, and no-one had the money to pay for its replacement. We immediately suggested he stay in our flat until I returned at the beginning of January.

The journey proceeded as usual and we were becoming inured to the crossing from East Germany. I left Braunschweig first in the new year and travelled to East Berlin alone. Heavy snow weighed down the branches of the fir trees and the temperature was well below zero even at midday. I had a two-hour wait for the Budapest train which was due to depart at 10 pm. I had no couchette, but the first class compartments were comfortable and usually uncrowded, so I thought I would be able to get some sleep. I was wrong. As I sat down by the window I realised that the temperature inside the train was the same as that outside. I kept my coat and made the overly-optimistic presumption that the heating would come on once the train began to move. Another three people joined me in the compartment and likewise began to complain about the lack of warmth.

The train pulled out of the Ostbahnhof and one of my fellow travellers extracted a bottle of cognac from his bag and passed it round. I accepted gratefully. It was a very long eighteen hours to Budapest and when I once walked to the restaurant car I found that snow which had come in through an open door had not even melted inside the train. More dramatically, I saw with total amazement that the Danube was completely frozen over at Esztergom, a cathedral town in the north of Hungary on the border with Czechoslovakia.

Laurence was waiting for me and confirmed that the Danube was also frozen in the city. Some people had walked right across though it was obviously risky. It would be another ten days before Paul returned, and as Laurence left we agreed he should call in to have baths and that we would go to a concert together a few days later. The freezing temperatures continued, the ice on the Danube was broken by ice-breakers, and on our way home after the concert our faces burned from the stinging cold of minus twenty degrees. Paul returned with the good news not only of having got his Ph.D., but that Cambridge University Press wanted to publish a version of his thesis as a book.

Gradually we were beginning to get to know the other people in the house. It seemed that every type was represented. On the ground floor of the courtyard was Pali bácsi, the wheelchair was his. He was probably about sixty years old, and could just manage to walk a short way with the aid of two walking-sticks. His daily outing was to the pub on the next corner, where in the good weather he would sit in his wheelchair on the dirty pavement, frequently accompanied by an obese, one-legged gypsy woman, also in a wheelchair.

On the first floor was the caretaker. She must have been of a similar age and was a confirmed alcoholic. She was thin and loud, and was frequently to be seen staggering along the walkway, bottle in hand. Also on the first floor, immediately beneath us, was a young couple with two children. They seemed very well off in comparison with the other residents, they had an Old English sheepdog, drove a western car and were always fashionably dressed. I could not imagine they would be staying in the house for long. I was proved right, though not in the way I had thought. Some months after we moved in, the man was arrested, the furniture was removed by bailiffs and the dog also disappeared. Shortly afterwards the woman and the children left too. We never learned the details.

On our own floor we knew more people. There was a gypsy family, a middle-aged couple with grown up children.

The man, also the worse for drink, was a restaurant violinist. Occasionally other gypsy musicians would appear carrying violins, clarinets and double-basses and the sound of their practising would echo around the courtyard.

Next door to them was another couple, the Molnárs, in their fifties, quite middle-class, with a weekend house out of Budapest near a river where he would regularly go fishing. Then came Mr. and Mrs. Varga, ourselves, and on the other side was an elderly Jewish couple. The husband had been ill and had difficulty walking and talking. We first became aware of him one day while we were sitting listening to a record of Vangelis's 'Chariots of Fire'. A slow-motion vision of an athlete shuffled past our net-curtained windows. They had obviously been told he should exercise, so every afternoon his wife dressed him up in a tracksuit, running shoes and peaked cap, and he walked at a snail's pace two or three times around the walkway. His wife followed, alternately encouraging him or exchanging gossip with her second-floor neighbours. We ever after referred to him as 'Chariots of Fire'.

Next to this couple was Ági néni, around sixty, who lived alone. She was also Jewish and had apparently been deported during the war and she had never recovered. Although she was extremely friendly and seemingly normal, she kept several plastic roses planted in soil in pots outside her door. Not only did she water them assiduously, I also saw her 'feed' them with paprika powder. She could also be observed in mini skirt and snow boots on her way to the local shop in the middle of July.

The next flat belonged to the couple with the telephone, and the door on the far opposite side of the courtyard to us belonged to a woman in her thirties, rough but good-hearted, with three poorly-dressed, though polite children. Mrs. Varga once whispered that not only had she never married, but each of the children had a different father. Certainly, they all looked very different.

We had still not got around to registering ourselves in the new flat with the council. It was to this end that Paul set off one day in January. Standing on the street corner of the council offices was a large, smartly dressed gypsy looking around searchingly. As Paul approached, the gypsy walked up to him, 'Do you know where Rigó Street is?' he asked.

'I don't know,' Paul replied. 'Unfortunately, I'm a foreigner.'

The gypsy looked in bewildered amazement, 'Unfortunately? Unfortunately?!' he burst out, laughing. Paul's word order had become muddled, he had meant to say, 'Unfortunately I don't know...' The gypsy was still laughing as Paul entered the building.

I had resumed cello lessons with Zoli and things were going well, although both his and our lack of a phone made arranging lessons difficult. He was nearing the end of his five years at the Music Academy and was considering two major changes in his life – marrying his girlfriend and leaving Hungary to work abroad. He both hated the bureaucracy of the government, and musically felt he would never achieve anything by staying. The best he could hope for was to play at the opera or in the state symphony orchestra, where as he put it, he would earn just enough to starve on and have to spend every spare minute teaching instead of practising. It was a complaint I had heard many times before.

Towards the end of April an English pianist friend, Danielle, arrived to see us. She had fallen in love with Hungary when she had come to see us in Garay Square. Since that time Ági and Kazi had gone to stay with her in London, and now it was Danielle's turn to be accommodated in their flat up the road. We were also expecting Sue, Steve and baby Tim to arrive halfway through Danielle's visit and we had decided that they should squeeze in with us.

It was at about this time that we decided to have a rather belated flat-warming party. Among our old friends we invited Miklós, János, Endre, Caroline, and newer ones like Ági and

Kazi and Virginia and Joseph – together with Virginia's Hungarian teacher, Eta. It provided an opportunity for people who had heard of one another but not met, to do so, and for Danielle to get to know our wider circle of friends. Towards the end of the evening dark-haired Eta stood on the steps of the gallery and made a surprise announcement: 'I'd just like to say how much I've enjoyed being here and getting to know some of you, and Pali – my husband – and I, would like to invite all of you to our place, near Ócsa, next Saturday.' It turned out that Pali was a vet, and he had been made a present of a road-kill deer, and Eta was intending to cook us all a venison dinner. We arranged that those with a car should meet at our flat from whence Pali would lead the convoy out to their home.

So the following Saturday, four or five carloads of people turned off the main road to Dabas and bumped their way along the track leading through woodland to an isolated house. Having greeted everyone, Eta led us into their sitting room, furnished in traditional peasant style and with a huge, blazing tiled stove. While the others were chatting and drinking the homemade pálinka and wine Pali had brought in, I went out to the kitchen. The table was covered with an array of dishes and tureens full of steaming food. I pointed to each, asking Eta for a description of what we were to eat. As I enquired about the third she smiled, a mischievous twinkle in her eyes, and said, 'Just taste it. I won't tell you what it is, I'm sure English people never eat it.' But my curiosity was aroused and I succeeded in persuading her to reveal the identity of the mystery delicacy. 'Testicle stew,' she said.

I thought I had misheard. 'What?'

'Yes, testicle *pörkölt*, it's very good – do you like kidneys?' I wrinkled up my nose. 'Well, then maybe you wouldn't like this either, but give it a try.'

I was still staring dubiously at this culinary revelation when the others arrived, ushered in by Eta, who took their plates and began to help themselves. As I saw Danielle take a generous spoonful of this improbable gastronomic delight, I wondered whether to warn her. I watched her out of the corner of my eye as she swallowed a mouthful of the stew.

'Good?' I asked.

She considered. 'Tastes like kidneys,' she replied, adding, 'Yes, very good.'

I simply could not resist it. 'Shall I tell you what it really is?' I asked. She nodded. 'Testicle stew.'

She stared with new insight at the food in front of her, and then without a word took a large gulp of wine, picked up her plate and disappeared out to the kitchen, soon returning with a new plate of what I had also chosen.

Paul worked day and night to get the book version of his thesis ready for publication. He did not put too much trust in the postal service and intended Sue and Steve to take the typescript back to Cambridge with them. Their letter said that they would be arriving on March 29th at 3 pm.

We decided that Sue and Steve should sleep in our bed up on the gallery and Tim should have the sofa underneath. We needed to buy another two mattresses for ourselves to sleep on the floor of the small area Paul used as a study. Somehow, everything had been left until the last minute, so we got up early to prepare for the day's main activities – buying the mattresses, going out to the airport, and later Danielle and Paul were going to the opera.

We walked out of the house to the trolley-bus stop. We waited for a quarter of an hour but no trolley came. Then some people walking past informed us that no public transport was running in the area and Dózsa György Street was sealed off while preparations were made for the April 4th parade – the anniversary of the liberation of Hungary from the Nazis by the Soviets at the end of the Second World War. Memories flooded back in both our minds, of an April 4th celebration we had been to in Józsa, near Hajdúböszörmény, where one of Miklós's brothers, János, ran a state farm.

It was the dark, wet evening of a blustery day we had spent

with János and his family. The discussion and arrangements concerning the evening were made in Hungarian, we knew only that there was to be some 'socialist celebration' at the farm. When we arrived there, a small crowd of people carrying umbrellas in the unlit lane were making ready to walk on up the road. We dodged the rivulets of water and patches of mud, walking with Miklós at the back of the procession, János having gone to the head with a wreath in his hands. A short way up the road we turned into a small cemetery, comprising five graves in total, each headstone bearing the red star, hammer and sickle. Together with one or two others, János stepped forward and placed a wreath on each of the graves – the graves of Russian soldiers. A few short speeches were made under dripping umbrellas, and then the crowd ambled back down the lane to what looked like a village hall. There we sat on wooden chairs and listened to interminable speeches about productivity and quota fulfilment, after which, outstanding workers were called up onto the platform where they received small bags of money and certificates in recognition of their achievements. It reminded me of a school prize-giving, except for the beer and the red star above the platform.

The mattress shop was on Dózsa György Street, so we began to walk hoping we might be able to find a taxi. We were in luck, we hailed the first one which passed though the driver seemed doubtful that we could drive all the way to the shop. However, we managed to stop in a small side street off Dózsa György and walked the rest of the way. We were in luck again, they had some mattresses. The shop assistant rolled them up, tied them with string and we carried them out to the waiting taxi. The driver got out of the car and the three of us began to try and force the mattresses into the back of the car. It was impossible. We paid what we owed, groaning inwardly at the long walk home.

The mattresses were not so much heavy as cumbersome, and the string cut into our hands. We had walked about halfway along a deserted Dózsa György Street when like a camel in the desert we saw a bus coming from behind us. We ran as best we could to the nearby bus stop but our hearts sank as we saw the bus was full to overflowing. The doors opened, we took a deep breath and shoved our mattresses into the mass of standing passengers. Some people were splayed up against the windows, others were pushed onto sitting passengers' laps, but we were on. The bus moved up the road to the next stop and opened its doors. It would have been physically impossible for anyone else to get on. But they were not going to – we had to get off, the remainder of Dózsa György Street was closed.

We walked the rest of the way home. I was slightly anxious about the time as the journey out to the airport on public transport was a good hour. Paul decided to make use of the afternoon to continue with his book, so I grabbed something to eat and left.

The airport building was airless and crowded. The plane had just landed and I waited for the first English people to come through from customs. After about twenty minutes no more people carrying luggage bearing British Airways stickers were in evidence. After a further twenty minutes I was worried. I went to the information desk. 'I'm expecting some friends from England on the B.A. flight, could you check if they were on the plane please?'

'I'm afraid we do not have a passenger list,' came the reply. 'Wait a little longer,' the woman suggested.

I returned to my seat. Another half hour passed with no sign of any English passengers. I went back to the information desk, 'Surely there must be some way of finding out if my friends were on the B.A. flight,' I began, 'it's half past four and the plane landed at three. They've got a young child, they don't speak a word of Hungarian and we don't have a phone so they can't contact us. I can't leave the airport until I know if they're here.'

'Just a minute,' said the woman, picking up a phone. 'What's their name?'

'Kearsey,' I replied. I waited.

'Yes, visas with that name have been handed in so they must be here. Why don't you go through to the customs hall and see if they're there?'

'Am I allowed?' I asked in surprise.

'It'll be alright. They must be there.'

I walked self-consciously through the automatic doors as they opened to allow some travellers out. One or two customs officials looked up but I was not challenged. I was surprised to see Lingua's accountant in the queue of people at the 'Something to declare' desk. I explained what I was doing there. 'Well, I was on the B.A. flight and I can tell you that there were quite definitely no children on the plane.'

I thanked him and went back. 'They're not there, and I've just spoken to someone who said there were no children on the flight. Could you check again?' She did. There were now no visas with their name on. I looked at the wall – five o'clock, I would have to rush home. I wondered what could possibly have gone wrong.

Back at Szinyei Street I ran up to Paul. 'They weren't on the plane, Tim must be ill or something. Maybe you can try and ring them from Ági and Kazi's after the opera?'

'I won't be able to go,' he replied. 'I'll have to send my book with Danielle instead of Sue and Steve and she's leaving in a week so I'll have to work.' Paul changed out of his suit while I quickly pulled on a dress. Danielle would be waiting. As I ran out of the flat past the letter boxes near the entrance, something caught my eye. I opened our post box to find a letter from Sue sent almost three weeks earlier. They had had to change their day of departure and were arriving the following day!

I ran back upstairs and relayed the information to Paul. It was six thirty and the performance was starting at seven, Paul changed back into his suit and bolted out of the door. I wondered if public transport would now be back to normal. One hour later he and Danielle appeared at the front door – due to illness the performance had been cancelled.

As I returned to the airport the following afternoon I hoped fervently that the same woman would not be at the information desk. I was sure she would think I spent my free afternoons scouring the place for non-existent friends, and annoying airport staff. I arrived at three o'clock to find Sue and Steve already waiting – I had forgotten that the clocks had been put forward the previous night. They had landed an hour earlier.

In spite of some trepidation on their part, their stay went well. We had recommended they bring their backpack to take Tim around, something still unknown in Hungary. They were surprised at the Hungarian obsession with children. Tim was constantly chatted to, given biscuits and smiled at on trams and underground, while Sue and Steve were frequently asked if Tim were really comfortable in his backpack. We took them with us for lunch at a restaurant, together with Márta, János their son András and Danielle. Tim happily wandered around the tables being talked to by other people eating there and was given a guided tour of the kitchens by one of the waiters.

Back at the flat we had problems with the front door. The key turned in the lock but the door would not open. The only solution was to leave a window open and climb in from the walkway outside. Anywhere else this might have been regarded as an open invitation to burglary, but crime in Budapest was rare. We had not personally met anyone who had been burgled, and we had been amazed to learn that postmen brought pensioners' money in cash to their doors on the fifth of every month, along with the letters. They walked the streets carrying large quantities of money in their brown, leather bags.

Another aspect of living in such a building as ours was that it was impossible not to be seen down in the courtyard by eyes from every window. In the sunny weather it was customary for pensioners to sit on a stool on the walkway, surrounded by potted geraniums, talking to a neighbour, listening to the radio or reading the newspaper. No-one entered the courtyard unchallenged, no matter how politely. 'Who are you looking for young sir?' someone was sure to call down to the unsuspecting stranger. We often returned from teaching to be given a photofit description of some friend who had called to see us, together with a message of when he would come again. Leaving windows open posed no risk at all.

The comings and goings of not only the five of us, but various other friends, the gas-meter reader and Zoli with his cello, all through the window, provided a certain amount of entertainment for our neighbours. What was less amusing but more dramatic was when Danielle decided to try and jump through the window – unfortunately, the wrong one – and brought the gas radiator off the wall with her. It took several months to get it mended since spare parts were unavailable and we needed to find someone with contacts at the factory who could obtain the necessary parts.

The shopping around our new flat was disastrous. One small supermarket was all that existed within walking distance. It was dark, the assistants rude, and you could smell sour milk from the doorway. Taking empty bottles back was a constant problem, either they did not accept the particular type of bottle I wanted to return, or they would have done but they had no spare crates and told me to return the following day. In this event I was forced to go home again to empty my shopping bag of bottles, and return once more to the shop. I tried another supermarket near Ági and Kazi's but their bottle return hatch in the outside wall was closed. I had once tried throwing them in the dustbin but was berated by the neighbours from their vantage point on the walkway.

Thus, the kitchen floor was covered with neat lines of dusty bottles to the point where we could hardly move. Paul decided that the only solution was to throw them away late at night when everyone was asleep. He filled several large carrier bags and crept along the dark walkway and down the stairs. There happened to be one dustbin at the foot of the spiral staircase, which he silently opened. What he could not see in the dark though, was that the bin was completely empty, and as the first bottles crashed to the bottom the sound of breaking glass rang out around the courtyard. Lights snapped on and Paul beat a hasty retreat just as the completely paralytic caretaker lurched out of her door, bottle in hand, shouting, 'Who's that using my bin? That's my bin down there!' and then presumably calling to someone on the ground floor she continued, 'Laci, who's that using my bin? Laci!'

A door opened and a head emerged. The man ambled over to the bin, peered in and then shut it. 'It's alright,' he called, going back into his flat.

'Who was it?' shouted the caretaker, clutching the railing for support and peering down below. But no-one answered. She had not noticed Paul hiding in the shadows and as she staggered back inside, he ran up to the flat where he found me laughing helplessly. From that time on we put the bottles in with our other rubbish and they silently disappeared.

Something that was not going to be disposed of so easily was our old car. We had already heard from Miklós's brother Dani that the presence of a right-hand drive, western-made vehicle had excited the curiosity of the local police. When challenged, Dani had stated that the car belonged to his wife. The police duly made a note of the fact that Dani's spouse was one Paul Merrick. Following this, the English M.O.T. certificate expired. In Hungary however, such a certificate was issued for three years, so that the obvious solution presented itself of forging a new date on the original paper. I did so, gaining another two years' grace before we would have to get it through a Hungarian M.O.T.

However, the car was now rusting badly, the steering column was gradually parting company from the chassis, and Dani felt it was not worth the cost of repairing. It was fourteen years old and had 200,000 miles on the clock, though the engine was fine. We agreed to go on the train to Debrecen and bring the car back to Budapest, Dani seemed to think we could still sell it. There was, however, one major obstacle we had not foreseen. We should, apparently, have declared our possession of the car to the customs. All the information concerning the car was contained on our original 30-day visa forms with which we had entered the country, so we had not considered it necessary, and no-one had ever asked. Had we declared it, we would have been issued with a new number-plate and documents which we now did not have. Even with such papers it would also have been impossible to sell the car, as it would have been entered onto the same list as our record-player and other 'valuables', in the National Bank. None of our possessions could be sold and they would be checked when we left the country. Whoever we approached flatly refused even to consider buying a car without papers. Furthermore, we could not take the car out of the country without them either.

Endre offered to let us keep the car at the side of his house which at least avoided more parts being stolen, and more importantly the possible enquiries of an over-zealous police-man. Miklós, for his part, offered some good advice, 'Tell everyone you can trust, someone's bound to come up with an idea. Every problem has a solution,' he said reassuringly. As usual, he was right.

One of my students in the Foreign Trade College group, who also worked at the Ministry of Foreign Trade, had a colleague who was very interested in the car. We met, arranged a time for him to see the car and agreed a price. I asked him about the lack of papers. 'Don't worry,' he said. 'I've got a friend at the customs who will give me false papers. I'll probably take the engine out and use it in my Beetle, and then scrap the rest.' And so he did, and we never heard anything about the car again.

It was towards the end of the Lingua term when I was greeted by a stocky Hungarian as I came out of the classrom at the end of one of my lessons. 'Are you Marion?' he asked. I nodded. 'I'm Attila,' he said, holding out his hand. 'My wife is having English lessons here. I've just come back to live in Hungary – I left in '56 when I was sixteen,' he added.

'Nice to meet you,' I said, shaking his hand.

'I just wanted to ask you if there's anything you'd like from England, or anything you want to send,' he continued. 'I drive over about every six weeks, so I could bring something if you need it.'

'That would be great,' I replied, 'but can I contact you in a day or so, I need some time to think?'

'Just give Anna the list,' he said, 'and give me your phone number. We don't have one.'

'Nor do we,' I laughed.

Two days later I gave my shopping list to Anna, which included some of the usual things we brought back ourselves in the summer such as tea-bags, soap, some herbs and spices, sellotape that would stick and ballpoint pens that would write. Attila returned some five weeks later and called in with not only what I had asked for, but some Stilton cheese and a bottle of sherry. This marked the beginning of a long friendship.

Another new friendship began very soon afterwards. We were contacted to do a recording at the Pannonia film studios, a voice-over for some advertisements. As we walked into the sound technicians' room we heard the very distinctive, gruff voice of someone doing an ice-cream advertisement. This was Harvey, Mr. Harvey as the technicians called him. He only had one sentence to do but the producer had very definite ideas about how it should be done. It seemed fairly obvious to me that Harvey's laughter would soon turn to hysterics unless he had a break.

'Let's have a coffee,' said the producer, reading my thoughts. We adjourned to the café and found that Harvey had been in Hungary quite a few years already and was married to Régina, a doctor and a specialist in rheumatism.

He also had two young sons. Before we left that day he had invited us to visit them at the weekend.

June in Hungary is the month of exams and school-leaving celebrations. Especially in secondary schools, though in primary and even nursery schools, traditional celebrations are held to mark the rite of passage from one school to the next. Teenage boys wearing suits, girls in black skirts and white blouses and parents in elegant attire can be spotted all around the country at any time in May or June. Relatives, parents and friends, laden with bouquets of flowers, make their way to say their final farewells to school friends and teachers. It is also the tradition for pupils leaving school to go to the homes of their teachers and serenade them. Thus it was, that one evening sitting in our flat, we heard singing resounding around the courtyard. Looking up I saw a group of students I had taught at Lingua, standing on the walkway, outside our windows.

Among them was Geoff – another Zoli in real life, but it was Lingua's tradition to give their students English names. He was quite the most gifted student I had taught and would now be going on to do an English degree at Budapest's ELTE university. His parents were both musicians and quite coincidentally lived in the same block of flats as Lingua. His mother had been the one who had arranged Paul's job and work permit, in her capacity as personnel officer at the Music Academy. They had become a second family to us and I often went down from the sixth floor at Lingua to their second-floor flat when I had time between or after lessons. They had witnessed my first, faltering attempts to speak Hungarian and had not been able to stop themselves laughing, though they were always patient and encouraging. Little did I then realise that some five years later Geoff and I would be teaching together as colleagues.

My cello teacher Zoli was also leaving the Academy as was Paul's erstwhile student Tamás, who used to swap recipes with him. Zoli, now married, had managed to get a job

145

playing in a palm-court orchestra on an island off West Germany called Borkum. It was sad to lose him both as a teacher and a friend, though he promised to find me another cello teacher and to keep in touch. Meanwhile Tamás had no chance of passing his English exam, and without it would not be awarded his diploma. He arrived one evening to beg us to give him private lessons, something Paul had so far not done for anyone, fearing the deluge that would ensue if word got round. 'I can't pay you for the lessons,' Tamás explained, 'but I can come and clean your flat, cook, anything you like...' It was impossible to refuse. We agreed that the 'fee' for the lesson would be to play to us afterwards. He was intending to play the Tchaikovsky violin concerto for his diploma recital and suggested playing it at the end of one of his lessons with us. The lack of either an orchestra or piano led us to suggest that we should sing the orchestral interludes. Our enthusiastic, though increasingly frantic attempts, caused Tamás to break into uncontrollable laughter.

Temperatures began to soar as June turned to July and we prepared for our annual visit to England. Laurence was also spending the summer with his parents and we agreed to spend a few days together during the holiday. We visited Sue and Steve in Cambridge, now with a second baby, our parents, and other relatives and friends. Then we travelled to Chester where Laurence picked us up and drove us to his parents' house on the English-Welsh border. His father, George Roman, was the director of Welsh National Theatre, and his mother Judy was completing work on her thesis for a Ph.D. in philosophy. When they left Hungary in 1956 they spoke hardly a word of English but they were an extremely talented family. Laurence himself was busy finishing an opera commissioned by English National Opera, and after his year as a composition student at the Liszt Academy, had been asked to teach composition there. We spent three memorable days in their company, playing through the whole of Laurence's opera to George in one of the theatre's practice-rooms, eating Judy's wonderful creations and having passionate discussions about Hungary with George.

We returned to Budapest early in September and began teaching almost at once. It was still very warm and we looked forward to more autumnal weather. Spring and autumn were usually short and often rainy, though it was rare for a day to pass quite without sunshine. Most Hungarians hate rain and were ill-prepared for it when it came. They always reminded me of cats gingerly picking their way through the puddles – often with plastic bags over their hair in lieu of an umbrella.

Late in October I bumped into Caroline in the street. 'I'm glad I've met you,' she said, 'I was going to write you a postcard inviting you both to our Guy Fawkes party. We always have one for the boys. Of course we can't get fireworks, but we make a guy and a bonfire and I've got some sparklers left from last Christmas.' The party was on the Saturday after the 5th of November, and two other English families came with their young children who gleefully drew patterns in the dark with their sparklers while we drank hot mugs of curried apple soup.

'Have you done this every year?' I asked Caroline as we stood by the fire.

'Yes. But we nearly got into trouble a year or two after we started,' she replied. 'Our neighbours came round and said if we didn't stop doing this every year they would go to the police.'

'Why?' I asked incredulously.

'They thought that the guy, with his moustache, was Lenin, and since Guy Fawkes is so near to November 7th they assumed we were burning Lenin on the bonfire every year,' she said. 'I had to give them a quick English history lesson to avoid being reported.'

Miklós and János had persuaded me to do a week's teaching on a new course at a state farm in a village near the Romanian border called Mezőhegyes. 'Now, you'll have to catch three trains to get there,' explained Miklós. 'First you go to Békéscsaba, change and catch the train to Orosháza which you've done before, and from there you get the train to Battonya which stops in Mezöhegyes. One of the students, a vet called Laci, will meet you at the station.'

It was already late November when I went. By the time I arrived in Békéscsaba it was dusk and once in Orosháza it was pitch black. I found the Battonya train and hauled my bags of books up from the ground below. As usual in country stations there were no platforms. We pulled out of Orosháza station, stopping again some ten minutes later. I peered out into the total blackness thinking the signal must be red. But no, doors slammed, people got off and others on with no sign of a building, a light or human habitation in sight. The train was now quite crowded with country people carrying bags of food and wine, and one with a duck or possibly a goose which occasionally stuck its head out of the covered basket in which it was being transported.

Again the train stopped in the middle of nowhere. Turning to a fellow-passenger I asked, 'Is this Mezöhegyes?'

'No, not yet,' came the reply.

'Do you know how many more stops it is?' I asked again, fearful of missing it altogether.

The woman turned to someone else, 'How many stops to Mezöhegyes?' she asked in turn. The other shrugged. He did not know how many stops it was but he said he would tell me when we got there. Every time the train slowed down I looked with anticipation at the elderly man until he finally nodded, 'This is it.'

There was only one person waiting on the platform so I boldly walked up to him and enquired whether he was Laci the vet. He was. He spoke Hungarian with alarming velocity but I had long ago mastered the art of nodding in the right places, so I settled myself in the car while he drove to the farm's holiday-home where I would be staying. It was a small, low building with about six rooms, and after depositing my bags we continued to his home. There I met his wife Alice, who was also on the language course, and their two sons. Alice spoke quite reasonable English, so in a mixture of both languages we had a good supper together, which was then interrupted by a knock at the kitchen door. It was a man from the farm to say Laci was needed to assist at a calving, the car was waiting outside. Of course, I reminded myself, no phone. In fact I later learned that only the doctor had a phone and only one public telephone existed in the whole village.

Standing up and looking at me Laci asked, 'Coming?' I nodded, leaving my unfinished wine and waving a quick goodbye to Alice. We were driven at speed over a bumpy, unmade road towards nothing more than a faint glow in the distance, finally stopping at a large farm outbuilding. Inside, it was warm and damp, and as we walked towards the men surrounding a groaning cow at the far end of the barn I saw a cat nursing its kittens in the straw of an empty stall.

Laci's friendly, easy-going manner changed instantly as he rattled out orders to the men, rolling up his sleeves to examine the cow. I was given to understand that it was to be a Caesarian, but that it is dangerous for cows to lie down and they can therefore only be given local anaesthetic. The cow's flank was sprayed, several injections given, and then Laci made the first incision through the cow's hide. Following this, he had to cut through layers of muscle. It was at this point in the proceedings that I began to feel strange. I am not squeamish, but the sight of the cow turning to watch itself being cut open proved too much, and I realised I was about to faint. I came round a few minutes later in a small area off the main barn, sitting on a bale of straw in the company of the man who must have carried me there. He stood grinning at me and offered me a glass of water. Luckily, I felt well enough to walk back in time to see the calf emerge from its mother, now too preoccupied with her offspring to take any notice of the stitching in which Laci was engrossed.

I remained in Mezőhegyes for a week, soon becoming accustomed to being whispered about by passing schoolchildren, ('That's the English lady!') as we passed one another in the small park on my way to where our lessons were held. My evenings were invariably spent with Laci and Alice and sometimes other members of the group would join us. On the Saturday which marked my departure there was to be a pig killing – traditional in the weeks before Christmas – at a friend of Laci's. As the vet, he had offered to commit the terrible deed – the pig was usually bled to death. I arrived at Laci's later in the morning to find Alice washing the pig's intestines in the sink ready for filling with minced meat for sausages. The kitchen floor was covered with deep trays of meat to which was added paprika, salt, pepper, garlic and blood. The mixture was then stuffed into the intestines, and a winter store of food was made. My only contribution was to peel and press the garlic, a generous one in view of the fact that my hands smelt for days afterwards.

Back in Budapest and at Lingua, new groups had been started. One of mine contained a man who proudly told me that he worked for the Hungarian Meat Trust. He asked me once, confident of an affirmative reply, whether Hungarian meat wasn't of the very best quality. I assured him that it was, but added that I missed eating lamb and had so far failed to find it at any butcher's shop.

'But you can get it anywhere!' he protested.

'Where?'

'All over the place!' he repeated.

I decided not to press him further.

Some nights later I was teaching my favourite group of students, including Geoff, all of whom were reaching the end of their school days and preparing for university entrance. There was a knock at the door, and when I opened it I saw my man from the Meat Trust standing in the corridor. 'Hallo,' I said. 'Your group is tomorrow, Wednesday, not tonight.'

'Sorry to disturb you,' he said. 'I've just brought you this,' he continued holding a large, white carrier bag out towards me. I took it from him, surprised by its weight.

'What is it?' I asked.

'Half a lamb,' he replied. 'Five kilos. I hope you like it,' he added, as he saw the dumfounded look on my face. I had rudely forgotten to thank him in my sheer amazement, and the perplexity of calculating how I would fit five kilos of lamb into a freezer the size of a shoebox.

'Thank you,' I stammered, 'thank you very much.' He smiled and turned towards the lift, as I walked back into the classroom clutching the bag. 'But what shall I do with it all?' I asked my laughing students. But then I had an idea. One of the group was a Piarist novice who lived in the town in a Catholic school which housed other monks. 'You take half of it,' I told him. 'Get them to cook it for you, I can't possibly use all this meat.' I cooked my half and invited Geoff, who had never eaten roast lamb before, though we had to make do without the mint sauce.

Christmas came and went with our customary journey to Germany. Mrs. Varga came out to greet us when we returned. As we exchanged pleasantries I noticed that the Molnár's flat next-door to her not only had its curtains drawn, but a large padlock on the front door and some sort of official-looking notice stuck above it.

'What's that?' I asked, nodding in the direction of her neighbours. She paused.

'They died over Christmas,' she said.

'What? Both of them?' I asked in amazement.

'Yes. Their chimney hadn't been cleaned and all the gases from the tiled stove came back into the room. Their daughter found them on Christmas day. He was sitting in the chair, a book on his lap, and she still had her knitting beside her. The council came and locked the place up. Terrible.' She was obviously upset, so we just nodded silently and let ourselves in the front door. When I met Miklós some days later I found his aunt and uncle had both also died in identical circumstances.

Just one year previously Laurence had been staying in our flat. Since then he had moved to a flat near Orczy Square, a market square with a similar reputation to Garay Square. He was now installed on the thirteenth floor of a fifteen-floor block and we paid him a visit as soon as he returned from Christmas in England. Laurence was by now teaching composition at the Music Academy and was also involved in teaching students at the College of Theatre and Film.

It was snowing as we left our building in Szinyei Street to walk to the 33 bus stop. As we made our way up the street we suddenly saw a notice on a metal stand, right in the middle of the path saying: DANGER! We looked around. No road works, gas works, holes in the pavement, in short, nothing dangerous at all that we could see. We walked on, still puzzled.

When we reached Laurence's flat we were surprised to see him arrive at the door wearing only a pair of swimming trunks, and with his balcony door wide open. However, as we walked in the heat hit us, it must have been 28 degrees. The centralised heating system which supplies most housing estates of this kind was notorious for the variability of heat supplied to different buildings, according to their distance from the heating plant. Added to the fact that Laurence was presumably close to the source of power, his proximity to the top of the building was turning his flat into an inferno.

He had brought a good supply of mince pies and Christmas puddings with him from England which we readily devoured in the tropical temperatures, exchanging stories of our Christmas travels, and his plans for compositions. We had been meeting regularly since we had first met, often cheering one another up with the aid of our shared, English and rather flippant sense of humour – often the only antidote to the illogical and absurd difficulties of everyday life. Laurence had been able to speak Hungarian when he arrived, having learnt it from his grandmother, who had also left for England in 1956 but had never learnt English. However, Laurence's new-found Hungarian friends were apt to fall about in fits of laughter when he came out with expressions or slang which his grandmother had presumably picked up in the 20's and 30's. We envied the ease with which he slipped from one language to the other.

On the whole, we had all managed to steer clear of a certain type of Hungarian who liked to associate with foreigners, sometimes in order to procure goods unavailable in Hungary, or to be invited abroad on holiday, but sometimes just to have a kind of status symbol in tow. It was under such circumstances that the three of us were invited to a party of well-to-do, self-employed people, the Hungarian equivalent of yuppies. We were very reluctant, trying every possible excuse we could come up with, but to no avail. Laurence's acquaintances had obviously ear-marked us all as the star attraction for their guests and were not to be put off. Laurence was particularly irritated since he felt certain they knew all our excuses were just that, and still they chose to force us to accept the invitation in the knowledge that we did not want to go.

A few days before the party we came up with the idea that we would pretend we had a recording job at the radio from 10 pm. – recordings were often done at night – and so we could leave at 9.30, hopefully having had some food but thus escaping the boring 'interview' stage to which we would inevitably be subjected later.

Laurence came to our flat and we made our way together to the dreaded event. Walking along Szinyei Street Laurence stopped at the sight of the DANGER! notice which was still there, but which we now passed daily without a second thought. 'No, we don't know what it's here for either,' I said, anticipating his comment. He looked around, then up. We followed his gaze. Up above us on the second floor of the building was a balcony, hanging precariously at an angle of some 30 degrees from the main structure. There was not even a cordon to keep anyone from walking, at their peril, immediately beneath the ton of cement and plaster.

When we arrived at the party a few elegantly dressed men and women were already sitting talking. We were introduced

153

to everyone and sat in the middle of the sofa. We felt totally out of place. At least I had a dress on, but Laurence in jeans and T-shirt looked as if he were trying to make a point. As there was no sign of food yet, we accepted drinks and began to answer the barrage of questions. 'But do you mean you really like living here?' one woman asked. 'Where exactly do you live in Budapest?' asked another. Laurence's mention of Orczy Square was greeted with an embarrassed smile and followed by silence. I looked at the beautiful, antique clock on the wall. Only eight o'clock. 'Did you go away for Christmas?' a man asked, seeming unconcerned which one of us should answer.

'Yes, we travelled to Germany,' I replied,

'And I was at home in Wales,' said Laurence.

'Do you ski?' continued the man looking at Paul.

'I'm afraid not,' he replied.

Yes, that was what had struck me about all the people here, I thought. They were all sun-tanned in February, presumably they had all been skiing, or to a solarium.

The inevitable questions about work and the like continued, while we stole impatient glances in the direction of the kitchen to see if any food would be forthcoming. We had already explained our sad intention of leaving the party at 9.30 pm. to our hosts the previous week, and now we mentioned it to the other guests. 'Oh dear what a pity,' said the woman in a short, pink dress with huge, black polka-dots on it.

'But how long will the job take?' asked someone else, 'Surely you could come back afterwards?'

'Oh you can never tell,' said Paul, 'we just have to stay until it finishes.'

'But we'll be partying till 4 or 5 am,' our host broke in, 'you must come back when you've finished. Yes, I insist.' There seemed to be no escape.

The time wore on slowly, the food only arriving about ten minutes before we had to leave. Trying to look suitably fed up and bored by the idea of working on a Saturday night, we

154

bade our farewells to everyone and walked out onto the cold, dark street.

'Now, what?' I asked.

'Let's go to your place,' said Laurence, 'Have you got any food at home, I'm starving!'

'But what shall we do about going back?' asked Paul. 'I'm not going back.'

'I know,' said Laurence, 'we'll ring them up later, pretend we're in the studio, and say everything's gone wrong – you know, faulty equipment, lost script, usual kind of thing, and that we'll be there for hours.'

Back in our flat we had some food and wine, wondering when would be a good time to telephone. Luckily, the nearest phone to our flat was working. Laurence volunteered to make the call in Hungarian. 'Yes, it's Laurence here, I'm ringing you from the radio. No, we haven't finished – the sound engineers arrived late, one of the microphones isn't working and now we find a page of the script hasn't been translated so I'll have to do it..., Yes, typical, isn't it? We're really fed up with it.' Paul and I tried hard to smother our laughter at Laurence's award-winning performance. But then, quite without warning, an ambulance rounded the corner, its siren screeching. Now the game would be up, surely. 'What's that?' shouted Laurence into the receiver, 'yes, not even the telephone in the studio works, so we had to come out onto the street to make this call while the engineers are trying to sort out the mike,' he quickly ad-libbed. When he put the receiver down we all squeezed back out of the phone box and laughingly accompanied Laurence to the bus stop.

A few weeks later I returned home from teaching to see our street alive with people at nine o'clock in the evening. Of course, lomtalanítás – once or twice a year residents may put out on the pavement all their rubbish of the type not usually removed by the refuse collectors – old furniture, pipes, broken electrical gadgets, bicycle wheels, car batteries... any and every imaginable thing. The dates for collection for any given area are published in the newspaper, and hoards of 'professional' scavengers make it their business to be there from the moment the first piles are dumped at the roadside. They moved methodically from one untidy heap to the next, carefully sifting through every item, extracting anything they could either use or sell. In the evening they brought torches, and like moles, scrabbled away in the darkness, their weak torch beams like faint glow-worms in the gloom.

As I passed the building next to ours there was a shout from above. 'Hey you! Leave that stuff alone, it's mine!' came the man's voice. It turned out that he was moving, and the pile of boxes and dilapidated furniture were what he was taking up to his new flat. The man he had addressed reluctantly replaced his new-found treasure on top of the pile, and ambled off to the next heap, pushing an already heavily laden, rusty pram with bent wheels in front of him.

★ ★ ★ ★ ★

It was nearly Easter. 'Well, are you coming to Böszörmény this year?' Miklós asked me when we next met at Lingua. It had been a year or two since we had been, but it never failed to revive the vivid memories of our first real holiday in Hungary, the Easter of 1980, two years after Paul's two-month British Council stay. Little had we realised that in Miklós's family it was at least as big a celebration as Christmas.

His immediate family consisted of himself, six brothers, one sister, and his now elderly parents. Miklós was the only member of the family to have left the area. Apart from his younger brother Dani, all the siblings were married with their own families, and Easter was the one time of year when they all gathered together. Their numbers were swelled by one or two cousins, godparents and a maiden aunt. The total number was around thirty-five.

Miklós's parents lived in what we later found to be a typical, small country house. It was built on one level and stood at right-angles to the road. Thus, going through the large, old, wooden gate you stood at one end of the house, the main door being halfway along. The roof overhung the entire length of the building, creating a ground-level verandah, shady and cool in the summer. Grapevines stood neatly tied to a fence alongside some colourful, untidy flowers, and from somewhere right at the other end of the house came the sounds of grunting pigs and clucking hens. Two thin, grubby cats lurked near the kitchen door as we approached.

Miklós's family was Greek Catholic and Easter was an important religious festival for them. They had already baked large loaves of 'kalács' (a kind of milk bread) each with what looked like five flowers in the dough, representing the five wounds of Christ, as we were later told. Those attending church on Easter Sunday morning took their bread to be blessed. The lamb which had been in the garden two days prior to Easter, had disappeared on the Saturday. When I asked what had happened to it I was led to the kitchen where, by way of an answer, Miklós's mother pointed to the largest saucepan I had ever seen, sitting on the small stove.

The only door into the house led straight into the kitchen from where opened a door on either side into the only two rooms in the house. Both rooms had a table stretching the entire length. Everyone arrived, formally dressed, the women crowding into the small kitchen to help, the men and children talking and laughing outside. Lunch consisted of giant tureens of chicken and vegetable soup with fine noodles, roast chicken, lamb (stuffed with egg), potatoes, and then plate upon plate of many kinds of cake, the entire meal accompanied by equally generous amounts of wine and beer. Following the meal, the children ran outside to play, the women gossiped as they washed up in the kitchen, and the men reminisced on this and that, still drinking, a few smoking.

Easter Monday was taken up with a traditional, Hungarian folk custom. The girls and women paint and dye eggs; men, alone or in groups, together with their sons, go to visit all their female friends and relatives. Arriving at the home of a girl they recite a short poem, usually about a flower wilting in the forest, and ask permission to water it. Permission given, the boy sprinkles the girl's head with water or cologne and she in turn gives him one of the eggs she has dyed. This is, in fact, a rather genteel version of the original custom of dousing girls with buckets of water, though even today some boys arrive armed with a soda siphon. Men are also offered ham, eggs, kalács and cake to eat and of course pálinka to drink.

On our first such Easter Monday, Paul was taken off by the seven Molnár brothers and assorted children while I stayed with his mother, sister and her teenage daughter. By lunchtime my hair reeked of a dozen kinds of cologne. However, this proved a kind fate compared to Paul's. Miklós had told us that to refuse food or drink is offensive, and that as far as possible we should accept at least a small portion of whatever we were offered. Paul, anxious to follow this advice, had drunk the proffered glass – or three – of pálinka at every home the Molnár boys visited. It was thus that he returned firmly supported on both sides and only semi-conscious. He subsequently slept till the evening and felt only somewhat better by the next morning.

Village life – though Hajdúböszörmény is strictly speaking a town – was peaceful and calming. In the late afternoon, the day's work done, the elderly men in hats and with walking sticks, the women in boots and headscarves, would sit on the narrow, wooden benches outside their garden fences, surrounded by colourful flowers, the small ditch, sometimes with water, in front of them, and watch their friends and neighbours cycling or walking home from work. Some would stop and talk about the prices at the market, their grandchildren or their ailments, others would just wave in greeting as they cycled slowly by. Some women sat and completed embroidery in the late afternoon sun, often accompanied by neighbouring women similarly engaged.

Many what we would consider 'indoor' activities were carried on outside. Miklós's father, sister and brother-in-law usually sat in the garden on low stools next to the grapevines in the mid-morning, peeling potatoes and chatting about family matters. Birth, marriages and death were still the central events of life, of conversation, and the passing of one of their number was announced by the prolonged tolling of the church bell, a different chime for a man or a woman. There was never a sense of urgency. People strolled on the uneven pavements, horses and carts clattered past, their drivers asleep in the hay, the horse plodding his familiar way home, children with jugs walked to standpumps for water, cats dozed by open kitchen doors hoping for scraps and the cockerel crowed a dawn which had long since passed.

* * * * *

Back in Budapest I decided that I would have to do something about getting a washing machine. I went to the shop I had been to with Endre, automatically taking a basket as I went through the door. Not that I was intending to put my machine into the basket, but it was a kind of entrance-ticket to a shop – you simply could not go around any shop without one. There were even baskets in the record shop which, if you put a record in, prevented you from lifting up the handles, so the only strategy left was to tuck this unwieldy burden under your arm. Worse still, in the record shop near the Music Academy, you were not allowed anywhere near the discs. Having approached the counter and waited the customary four and a half minutes for the assistant to finish his chat or his coffee, you were asked what you wanted. Browsing was an alien concept in most bookshops and when you re-emerged onto the street you had a pretty good idea of what they did not have in stock, but little idea of what they did.

The washing machine problem was solved some days later when Kálmán, to whom I had mentioned my intention of procuring another second-hand one, arrived one evening with a present. It was a rather small rusty tub, square, with a lid that sat on the top, like an oversized saucepan. It had to be filled with water of the requisite temperature with buckets, the lid put on, and the timer set to the required number of minutes. It was then plugged into the wall and began to gyrate noisily. When it was finished you unplugged it, threw the dripping clothes into the bath, and then positioning a spout at the front of the machine over the drain in the floor, tipped it so that the water came out. It even made my mother's antiquated twin-tub look space-age, and like the machine in Garay Square this too found its final resting place in the bathroom when we later moved away.

Another feature of daily life was the schizophrenic attitude towards queueing. In many places it was necessary to queue three times. Once to ask for what you wanted, again at the till to pay, and a third time when you joined the line of people waiting to have their purchases wrapped. However, in offices or doctor's surgeries the procedure was quite different. The strategy was to position yourself as near as possible to the door, which usually meant standing, and then leaping forward as soon as the door opened. However, there were many variations on this game – walking straight in (with maybe a cursory knock) without any regard to the others waiting, pleading that your last train home was leaving in half an hour and you must be seen immediately, or saying that you merely wanted to ask a quick question of someone inside, but of course then having your whole case dealt with.

At the end of April we began to hear rumours that there had been a serious atomic explosion in the Soviet Union, and that radioactivity was spreading all over Europe. There was, as yet, nothing in the Hungarian media – it seemed that even Gorbachov's glaznost and perestroika had difficulty in coping with this turn of events – but the BBC World Service confirmed the story. Laurence called in the same day. 'Let's switch off the lights and see if we glow in the dark,' he suggested. Budapest was, within a day or two, a giant grapevine along which Chernobyl-related jokes passed back and forth. The British Embassy relayed guidelines about not eating leafy vegetables, while at the Lehel Square market the sign advertising atom erős paprika ['atomic strength paprika'] had had the first word crudely struck through, and in other parts of the market atombiztos ('radiation free') lettuces were to be had.

With May came the spring. To anyone from England the temperatures more closely resembled summer, but the sudden bursting into bud and flower of every plant, bush and tree, the almost hysterical fervour of birdsong and the surging renewal of life always made me think of Stravinsky's *Rite of Spring*. It could not have been the bright, crisp sun and gentle showers of England he had in mind when he wrote the work. I could now understand it in a way I never had before. The same was equally true for Kafka's novels.

It was with such thoughts in mind that I walked down Szinyei Street towards the underground one evening on my way to the opera house where I would meet Paul and Laurence. We had tickets for a performance of Mozart's Cosi fan Tutte. We usually bought tickets for the upper circle which gave an excellent view from the centre seats and at twenty forints it could be regarded as free. Through the side entrance and up the many flights of stairs, we arrived in the beautiful red plush and gilt surroundings of the third floor café and cloakrooms. Paul and Laurence had no coats, but I handed mine in, pocketing the ticket. As we strolled towards our seats I glanced casually at a pile of programmes the usherette had left on her chair by the door. The picture was of a garret scene, the title, La Boheme. I nudged Laurence and pointed at the programmes, 'What's she doing, selling Boheme programmes?' I asked. Then we heard our answer as the usherette spoke to another member of the audience while she examined his ticket, 'Yes, it's Boheme tonight – lovely opera – due to illness they can't do the Mozart, lovely opera Boheme...'

Laurence wasted no time, 'Is it La Boheme tonight?' he asked her.

'Yes, lovely opera...' she began before Laurence interrupted her.

'But I haven't come here to see Boheme. I bought tickets for Cosi fan Tutte,' he said.

'But it's such a lovely work...' she repeated pointlessly.

We had seen it many times. It was not as though we had wasted much money on the tickets, but it was disappointing. 'Come on,' said Paul, 'we might as well see it now that we're here. After all ,' he said, mimicking the usherette, 'it's a lovely opera...'.

It was a good performance, not surprisingly really considering that the Opera House had no substitutes for the major roles, so if someone was ill the standby opera was always La Boheme, the equivalent for a cancelled ballet performance being Swan Lake.

When the opera ended I joined the throng jostling to reach the counter by the cloakroom to reclaim their coats. I rummaged in my pocket for my ticket, it wasn't there. I felt in my other pocket – nothing. I knew I had not put it in my bag but I searched there also. No luck. I walked over to where Paul and Laurence stood chatting. 'I didn't give you my cloakroom ticket, did I?' I asked Paul. He shook his head.

'Oh dear, have you lost it?' asked Laurence. 'Let's go back and see if it's where we were sitting.'

We searched under the seats in our row and the ones in front and behind, but in vain.

'How will I get my coat back?' I asked.

'Don't worry,' replied Laurence. 'We'll hang about till nearly everyone's gone and explain the situation,' he said, leading the way back to the cloakroom. There were still a few people at the counter, returning opera glasses and putting on their coats. Few garments were left on the hooks behind and I could see my coat quite clearly. Laurence approached the cloakroom attendant. 'My friend here has lost her ticket...' he began.

'Then I can't help you,' the woman interrupted curtly.

'But I can see it,' I said, 'that one over there,' I pointed.

'Without your ticket I can't give it to you,' she said, automatically taking the tickets from someone else and fetching his coat.

'Look,' said Paul to me, 'we'll just wait until all the other coats have gone and then she will know it's yours.' We stood in silence, waiting until the last of the audience had strolled away, but the woman ignored us and began to gather up her own belongings in preparation to leave.

'Look,' I said in desperation, 'my coat's still there, no-one's claimed it, and everyone's gone home, who else's could it be?'

She continued putting on her own coat and scarf as though she had not heard me. 'Don't you remember what number was on the ticket?' she asked, without so much as looking at me.

'No.' I had to admit.

'Well, how do I know it's yours then?' she asked.

'Who else's could it be?' asked Laurence, impatience now much in evidence in his voice.

'Maybe you dropped it where you were sitting,' she said.

'We've looked,' said Paul.

'Isn't it in your bag?' she asked, as though I wouldn't already have checked there.

'No, it's not,' I replied. She sighed.

'We're not leaving until we get the coat,' said Laurence.

She walked towards the old, corduroy coat, took it off the peg and unpinning the ticket plonked it in front of me. Then, without a word, she picked up her bag and walked off.

Some days later we were sitting in our flat having our evening meal with Laurence when there was a knock on the front door. Paul went to open it and we heard him saying, 'Hallo József, come in.' It was our landlord. He usually only came for the rent and had been just the previous week. Paul introduced him to Laurence while I cleared away the plates to the kitchen. 'We're thinking of selling the flat,' I heard József say as I returned with the coffee, 'and I wanted to give you time to find another place and let you know that we may bring people interested in buying it to see around the place.'

My heart sank. Although I wasn't particularly keen on Szinyei Street, nor this particular building, I liked the flat now and the idea of moving again was unappealing. Maybe even the actual move would not be so bad, but to find a suitable flat we could afford might take months. We did not want to live out in the suburbs and we needed a place which had plenty of space for all our records, books and other belongings. Before moving to Garay Square we had been to see one or two flats belonging to people who were going abroad for a year, but they were crammed full with their own things and we would have had nowhere to put ours. We agreed to try and move out at the beginning of September, but with the six weeks we were to spend in England, this did not leave us a lot of time.

The following Monday morning at eight o'clock I made my way up Szondy Street to Ági's and Kazi's. I taught them regularly since they both needed English in their jobs. As I turned into the gateway of their building Ági caught up with me. She had just taken the children to school a couple of streets away. 'How are you?' she asked.

'Fine,' I replied, 'but just imagine, we have to leave our flat, the landlord wants to sell it.'

'When do you have to move?'

'At the beginning of September,' I said.

We walked up to the first floor. She let me in through the glass doors which opened onto a small area off which three doors led into three flats. Once there had been only one flat here and these glass doors were the private entrance to the huge apartment which lay within. It had belonged to Kazi's family, and his elderly aunt still lived in a part of the original flat, now separated off and with its own entrance to the left of Ági's and Kazi's. The third door led into what they told me was a tiny flat occupied by a young couple with two children. In the 1950's the state appropriated all privately owned land and property, 'nationalising' it, and then proceeded to lay down new rules for how many square metres of living space must be occupied by what number of people. Thus, Kazi's family, like so many others, were forced to either leave or partition their large flats, or have the state foist total strangers on them to share their living quarters.

We walked inside. Kazi was waiting for us. 'Sorry, I can't stay this morning. I have to go into the office early – I'll see you next week.'

'You go in and sit down,' said Ági, 'I'll come in a minute.'

I walked into the huge sitting room. It was very imposing with its antique furniture, oil paintings and various objets d'art. The atmosphere of middle-class grandeur had survived the age which had sought to destroy it. I picked up the newspaper lying on the table, it confirmed my suspicions that although I might now be able to communicate reasonably in Hungarian, my knowledge was still no match for a newspaper.

Ági returned bringing two cups of coffee and sat opposite me on the Biedermeyer chair. 'So, what have you been doing this week?' I began, settling down to my coffee.

'We've got some exciting news!' she said animatedly. 'It looks like we are going to Brussels for a few years.'

'When?' I asked in surprise.

'Probably in August, so that the children will be able to start school at the beginning of September.'

'Will they go to a French-speaking school?' I asked.

'Yes. Perhaps I'll try and find someone just to teach them a few basic things before we go.' Ági went on to explain that the job, trade secretary at the Hungarian embassy in Brussels, would be hers. They would be given accommodation, the children could learn a second language, everything was perfect except for one thing. Kazi would have no work, in fact he would have to take care of the children and the household because Ági would be expected to work even if the children were unwell. At most, he could do some private business from home, or maybe, she added, he would work towards an M.A. 'And I've just told Kazi about your having to move, and we think you should come and live here,' she said.

I was flabbergasted. The thought had not occurred to me. We could never afford the rent for this flat of over one hundred square metres and they could easily find a wealthy foreigner who would be only too keen to rent it. I pointed out the obvious flaw in her plan.

'But if you don't come here we are not going to rent it out. We'd already decided not to, it's not worth the risk even for a high rent of having the furniture or other things damaged.'

'But we could hardly afford to pay you more than we're paying now,' I said.

'No problem,' she concluded. 'Talk to Paul about it. The only thing is that we will spend most of July and August in Hungary, so we would like to have the flat then, but you wouldn't have to pay rent for these two months.'

So it was that our problem was solved. More than that – we would have a beautiful flat near the park with a telephone and a working automatic washing machine, for the same rent as the Szinyei one.

We still had about six weeks before we planned to leave for the summer. Danielle had written from England to say she was coming for a couple of weeks and would be staying at Ági's and Kazi's. We had decided that we would travel with Laurence on the same plane back to England in the first part of July. However, Paul returned from the Academy one afternoon to tell me that one of the librarians there, a woman called Margó, had told him that she and her husband were intending to drive to England that summer and would be happy if we were to travel with them. When Paul explained our previous arrangement with Laurence she said without hesitation that he could join us too. She invited us all to their flat that weekend to discuss the idea with her husband, István.

We met Laurence and took the bus to Tüzoltó Street where István and Margó lived on the second floor of a small block of flats. We were welcomed very warmly and introduced to their two young children. Their living room was dominated by a huge aquarium where tropical fish in blues and turquoise darted between emerald green plants. We each told István something about ourselves and learned in turn that he taught law at the university. He had long wanted to visit England and they had now saved enough money to go. He quickly explained that he only had an eight-year-old Skoda, but he hoped it would get us there. Their children would stay with his parents, and they planned to go for a month, the maximum time allowed. He told us that he had a friend who lived in Freiberg in Bavaria and that we could spend a night or two there. So saying, he went to the bookshelf in the wall unit and brought out an atlas. It looked like a very long way to go in one day, though all of us except Margó could drive. 'I thought we'd leave at midnight and drive right through the next day until we get there,' said István. 'Then we'll spend the day in Freiberg and have a look around and go on to Paris the following day. We'd like to spend a day or two there before going to England. What do you think?'

We were all for it, and we had not been to Paris for a few years. The only question really was how we would return, as István and Margó would be travelling back before we intended to, but we left that question unresolved for the time being.

Danielle arrived some days later and was relieved to see the radiator re-attached to the wall of our flat. We met most days, but this time she was playing a lot with my cello teacher Zoli, and preparing for a concert with Tamás, so she was busy. She had also made a good friend of Attila's wife Anna, and met her both in Budapest, where she was working in a restaurant, and at their flat in Budakeszi. On one such occasion Danielle came back to Szinyei Street with Attila and Anna in the car and they both came in to see us. 'Would you like some tea?' I asked unnecessarily as soon as Attila sat down. He never refused.

'What kind?' he asked. 'An English tea? None of that continental mish-mash. Something you can stand your spoon up in.'

'Okay, okay,' I said. I knew by now that he liked his tea much stronger than even most English people, but producing it was not that straightforward with teabags designed to merely discolour the water. As I took the teapot in I heard Paul describing our proposed drive to England. Since Attila travelled back and forth every couple of months he was perfectly au fait with routes, distances and costs. 'So we're leaving here at dawn and driving to Freiberg in a day,' said Paul.

Attila raised an eyebrow. 'In a Skoda?' he queried. 'Five of you in a Skoda?'

'Don't you think that can be done?' I asked.

He let out a sigh. 'Well, all I can say, is rather you than me,' and he smiled. 'And how are you coming back?'

'Well, they can only stay away for a month, but we don't want to get back till the end of August... you're not going to be in England then, are you?' I asked hopefully.

'I don't think so,' Attila replied. 'But have you heard about the coach that goes from London to Budapest? You could come back on that, it's pretty cheap.' We had not heard about any such coach service. 'It's called 'Attila Tours' – nothing to do with me – but I know the man in London who runs it. He's Hungarian, and it's mainly intended for Hungarians to visit their relatives. I'm not sure how frequently it goes, but there must be quite a lot of runs in the summer months. Do you want me to find out for you?'

'Yes, that would be great,' we replied.

'Okay then, I'll call in and let you know in a few days.'

We had agreed to let Danielle stay in our flat while we were in England. She could not remain at Ági and Kazi's because they would be packing to leave, 'And anyway,' she said, 'I am

168

fed up with the water heater in their bathroom. It's impossible to get the temperature right. Either the water pressure is so low that the gas doesn't light or when it does it's scalding hot. Then, if you try to add a bit of cold water the flames go out again. I'd rather stay here.'

* * * * *

The weather was becoming increasingly hot. The glare of the sun reflected, glittering and sharp, from the tin gutters and pipes. There was no shade, no escape from its intense rays which bleached the tattered awnings of small, dark shops, softened the tar to a sticky goo, and when the wind blew, the dust stung your eyes and blackened your bare feet. I felt glad we were leaving, glad it would be dark and sunless when we departed at night. We could not take much luggage. Margó was taking a small camping stove and tins of ready meals for the journey. We had a final meeting a few days before we left. 'So, we will have a roof-rack,' said István, 'but please bring only what's absolutely necessary.'

'Well,' said Laurence, 'the only thing I insist on bringing is my opera. No, really,' he continued seeing our smiles, 'they wouldn't let me send it from the post office.'

'What are you talking about?' I asked.

'They asked me what was in the parcel, I had to fill a form in, and then they said they couldn't send it,' Laurence replied.

'But why not?'

'Because they said that it was a Hungarian work of art and you can't take a Hungarian work of art out of the country without a special permit from the National Bank or somewhere! We'll just have to hide it in the car!'

Margó shook her head disbelievingly. We discussed which ferry to go on, deciding on the Calais-Dover route, what presents to take for the couple in Freiberg and money matters: where to hide the forints we were also not allowed to take out, but which István and Margó would need for petrol or a possible emergency between the Austrian border and Budapest on the way home. 'The best thing is if we say we have a few hundred forints, but you say you don't,' said István. 'They won't believe us if we say we haven't got any at all.' I never really understood the problem of taking currency out of Hungary when, having crossed the border, it was as worthless as Monopoly money. Nevertheless, the regulation was strictly enforced.

István arrived at around 1 a.m. on the day of our departure, with Laurence already in the car. It was pleasantly warm now, and we soon began to doze once the initial, excited exchanges of our first hour in the car petered out. Two hours later we were awoken by István some miles before Hegyeshalom to see dawn breaking over the fields. We felt stiff and I yearned for some coffee. Apart from the odd farm vehicle there was little traffic on the country roads and no queue at the border crossing. We had to get out of the car while the guard looked at our passports and visas.

'Have you got any forints?' he asked.

'Yes.' 'No.' Paul and I answered simultaneously.

I gave him a wry smile. 'Nice one,' I muttered. The guard looked from one of us to the other.

'Let me see in your purse,' he said. I opened it, nothing but a few pounds. 'And yours,' he continued, looking at Paul. He opened his wallet to reveal about twice the allowed amount. The guard sighed. 'You can't take that out of the country.'

'So what can we do with it?' Paul asked.

'You'll have to spend it – there's a shop over there,' he said, indicating a small building behind us.

'We won't be a minute,' I said to István as we walked to the shop with Laurence. As we opened the door the aroma of strong coffee greeted us and instantly mollified me. We bought wine and chocolate as well as five coffees then returned, receipt in hand, to the waiting guard. 'Alright, you can go,' he grunted, waving us on.

The journey to Freiberg was uneventful and slow. István insisted on completing the whole drive himself with only a very few breaks. At lunchtime we cooked a tin of beans on the camping stove, at a lay-by on one of the motorways. We were refreshed after our nap in the back of the car. Laurence was on good form telling jokes and playing the fool, the atmosphere was like that of children beginning a long holiday from boarding school. So it was strange when I suddenly became aware of the cold stares of some Germans at a nearby table, sitting primly beside their immaculate Mercedes, eating unsmilingly, with an expression of incomprehension at the jollity of five – as they thought – Hungarians, in an old Skoda, so carefree yet so obviously poor.

We spent that night and the one following in Freiberg. We had an unscheduled evening in Rheims the next day as the distance to Paris was just that bit too far. The following afternoon in Paris, after much searching, we found a small, dubious-looking hotel near the eastern railway station. It was just about affordable though to have a shower was an extra ten francs, the key to the bathroom being kept at the reception desk on the ground floor. Our rooms were up a dark, rickety staircase on the third floor, the windows looked out onto similar establishments up and down the narrow street. It was stiflingly hot and humid, and after throwing off some of our clothes, we slept. Early in the evening we decided to go and eat, walk around the Eiffel Tower and come back for a shower.

Laurence sat on the end of my bed, idly twisting a coat hanger on one of his fingers while we waited for István and Margó. 'I can't wait to have a shower when we get back,' I said, pulling on my sandals.

'I reckon we could get away with just paying for two rounds,' said Laurence. 'You go with Margó, then Paul, István and I can probably squeeze in together, they'll never know.'

'Good idea,' I said looking up, just in time to see the coat hanger spin off Laurence's finger and go flying out of the window. We ran and looked out. Luckily his missile had failed to make contact with any passers-by, but as we watched we saw an Arab woman walk up briskly, pick the coat hanger up, and quickly looking all around, thrust it into her shopping bag.

We arrived back late. Laurence went to get the key for the shower, and he, Paul and István walked down to the first floor where the bathroom was located off the dining room. Some minutes later Margó and I heard Paul's unmistakable laughter. It was followed by a shout from Laurence. I wondered how long it would be before a member of the hotel staff would come and demand extra for the three showers. But no-one did. They were, we mused, probably too busy managing the more lucrative activities of the several semi-clad women we had seen who appeared to be permanent residents of the establishment.

We spent two days in Paris. I devoted the whole of one of them to finding Debussy's grave. It was not in the Pere Lachaise cemetry with those of other famous artists and musicians, but in a small out-of-the-way cemetery. We stood in the scorching midday sun and looked at the stark, black marble slab with its simple inscription: Claude Debussy, Musicien Français. I walked over to a nearby grave covered with red geraniums and took one pot. Then placing it on the middle of the tomb I said a silent thank you for the music I had loved more than any other since I was thirteen.

Around midnight on the second day in Paris we began to pack up to leave for the ferry. István was down in the street loading the roof-rack, Margó was checking she had not left anything, Paul and Laurence were chatting about music. Suddenly there was a whistle from the street. Margó went to the open window having recognised the whistle as István's. 'I've left the car keys up there somewhere, can one of you bring them down?' he shouted as discretely as he could, not wanting to wake the whole street at that hour. Laurence, seeing the keys on the bed next to him, stretched out and picked them up. Then, strolling lazily over to the window, he threw them down. It would have been a perfect shot, a good

172

landing, but for the gutter hidden in darkness on the second floor which neatly intercepted the keys. Margó, Paul and I stood speechless waiting for István's reaction but none came. He was waiting for the arrival of the keys by more orthodox means, and was unaware of the goings-on above him. Laurence seemed to have taken root to the spot. Then suddenly, he sprang to life, 'It's alright,' he said, unconvincingly, 'Margó, you go and tell István there's a slight hitch, while Paul and I go down to the second floor, to the room below us and ask them to let us in and get the keys out of the gutter.'

Margó left.

'You realise they're probably asleep?' I said to Laurence.

He smiled nervously and left the room with Paul. A moment later I followed them downstairs and heard them knocking at first politely, then more insistently. No luck.

'Maybe there's no-one there,' I said.

Laurence turned. 'You two keep trying and I'll see if I can explain the situation to the porter, then he'll probably let us in. What's the word for gutter?' Laurence asked.

'No idea,' said Paul.

'Just say they're outside the window,' I said trying to be helpful. Laurence wandered off practising his French. He must have succeeded because he soon returned with the porter who was brandishing a large bunch of keys. He too knocked loudly on the door, but to no avail. He shrugged his shoulders and put a key in the lock, then beckoning to Laurence they walked into the room. I could see by the lamp light from the street that someone was fast asleep but blissfully oblivious of the intruders. The window was open and the porter waited while Laurence half climbed out and began to grope about in the gutter. He was lucky. Triumphantly he held the keys up so we could see them. I shook my head and smiled. Typical. The porter locked the room again, leaving its silent occupant none the wiser as to his midnight visitors.

We spent most of the voyage from Calais dozing below deck, but patriotically went up to see the white cliffs of Dover as we approached the coast. Then we guided István to the west of London where he and Margó were to spend a few days with friends of ours, and from where Laurence's father was to pick him up and take him to their home in Wales, dropping us off in Reading en route.

We met both István and Margó and Laurence once during our stay, but we each had friends and families to visit and István his own itinerary to follow. We did get a phone call announcing their safe arrival back in Budapest, though the car had broken down in France somewhere. We also made arrangements with 'Attila Tours' for three seats on the coach back at the end of August with Laurence. We managed to see most of our friends including Danielle, who herself had returned from Hungary and was full of stories of a visit she had made to Transylvania just over the border into Romania. We saw Sue and Steve, now with a second baby boy called Laurie – after Laurence, whom they had met on their visit to us in Budapest. Just a few days before we were due to leave I thought I might be pregnant. I went to the local chemist's and bought a do-it-yourself pregnancy test. The result was positive. Paul and I were overjoyed, as was the rest of the family who had almost given up on grandchildren.

On the morning of our return to Hungary, we had to be in the east of London in a small side street at six in the morning. Luckily I felt fine, no morning sickness, though our pre-dawn departure would have been enough to bring it on. Laurence arrived a few minutes after us and on being told of our good news did a balletic pirouette in the middle of the road for joy. We soon realised that we were probably the only non-Hungarians using the coach, the other people lining up already munching salami sandwiches and speaking Hungarian. A stockily-built man was giving instructions about luggage and seating – he turned out to be the Attila of 'Attila Tours', more affectionately known as Leftie. We assumed that this was connected to his political persuasions, but later learnt that he was in fact left-handed!

It was a thirty-hour drive back to Budapest with several changes of driver but no real stop. The coach was comfortable but it was impossible to sleep. We were seated at the front, at the back the Hungarians were already in party spirit, joking noisily, smoking, laughing, eating. The only lull coming when we crossed the Austrian-Hungarian border.

Classes at Lingua began a few days later. We planned to move to our new flat ten days later at the end of August, though as yet we had not even begun to pack. I returned from my first day back teaching and realised with alarm that I was losing blood. I knew a gynaecologist, an Armenian called Marina, at St. John's Hospital, and Paul decided to try and phone her and ask her if she could come and see me. He ran out to Mrs. Nagy's flat, the only one with a telephone. The combination of the noise of the football match on the television in the adjacent room and the crackling of the ancient apparatus made any attempt at a discrete, intimate conversation an impossibility. As he tried to describe the situation to her he caught the Nagy's exchange glances. Before they could start to ask questions Paul thanked them and left. Marina had told him I should not get up and she would visit me the following day. It was a great relief to see her kind, smiling face and even more of a relief to hear that the baby was in no imminent danger, though apart from one visit, by taxi, to the hospital, I was condemned to stay in bed for two weeks. I could not remember having spent a day in bed since childhood. I was hot, I was restless and we had to pack. I tried to read. I listened to music, but became increasingly fractious.

In the meantime Paul contacted Miklós and said I would not be able to teach for a while. On his way home he bumped into Harvey who offered to move us in his car. Laurence dropped in and helped pack and finally we were ready to go. I was fine but not allowed to help. I was still confined to 'resting' most of the day. When I emerged from our flat for the first time in two weeks our neighbours were ready to say farewell, and with knowing looks and kindly smiles, to wish me the best of health. Harvey took me to the new flat first where I watched the gradual arrival of our boxes. Laurence came later in the evening just in time for a plate of the spaghetti Paul had made. We sat in the huge sitting room, surrounded by the antiques and large oil paintings.

'It's a bit like living in a museum,' mused Laurence.

'Well, you're welcome any time – without an entrance ticket,' laughed Paul.

I walked over to the window. It was dusk. Diagonally across the broad avenue of Dózsa György Square was the Museum of Fine Arts, and beyond it Heroes' Square and the City Park. On the other corner were the Botanical Gardens, a part of Budapest Zoo, and immediately opposite us was the "Chimneysweep' restaurant. Nothing had changed since our meal there with Endre that summer's evening two years and two flats previously. The same faded green trelliswork surrounded the tables in the garden, while strains of the same music, which always sounded the worse for drink, wafted up from the gypsy musicians playing in the deepening shadows of the small bandstand.

Children and Change
DÓZSA GYÖRGY STREET

Our new home combined grandeur with decayed elegance. The kitchen led off the entrance hall near the front door and then came the double doors into the sitting room. Another pair of doors led off from there to the bedroom and another pair to the third room, the three rooms adjoining one another in a straight line, though each could be entered also from the hall.

Unpacking was slow since the cupboards were almost full of Ági and Kazi's belongings. Eventually we managed to pack their things into our empty boxes which we stacked in the furthest room.

I had decided not to return to any regular teaching at Lingua, but continued to teach some children whose parents had worked as doctors in Libya. The children themselves had been to an international school where the language of tuition was English, so it was, for me, rather like being back at my school in England. They were bright and disciplined, it was obvious that they had no problems back at school in Hungary, and yet not one of them said they enjoyed school.

'Why not?' I asked in genuine surprise.

'It's so boring,' said one of the girls. 'I always finish the work halfway through the lesson and then I just have to sit there in silence for the rest of the time waiting for the others to finish.'

The youngest in the group, who had only just started school added, 'And I have to sit there learning the letters when I can already read...'

'And at the school in Libya we wrote our own poems and stories and acted in plays – here all we do is copy out of books!' a boy broke in.

It was sad that such obvious ability and enthusiasm were being stifled rather than encouraged.

We had, by now, met one of our immediate neighbours. Kazi's aunt, Marietta néni, lived in a flat even larger than our own, one of its rooms joining onto our sitting room: the wall separating the two rooms had not existed before the flat was divided. Despite being in her late seventies, she still worked every day as a physiotherapist at the National Institute for Rheumatology and was both lively and enthusiastic about her work. Obviously it was this that kept her so fit. She invited us into her flat one day: 'Yes, that's what we had to build,' she said pointing at the unfamiliar side of the wall whose other side we knew very well. 'This was one, huge room leading all the way to the conservatory here at the front,' she continued, walking ahead of us. A wall of glass separated her sitting room from the conservatory beyond and we walked through its glass doors into a jungle of potted palms and plants, and looked through the huge windows which faced directly onto Dózsa György Street and the botanical gardens. 'The whole of this first floor belonged to the man who built the house. He owned the Budapest circus.' This was just the other side of the botanical gardens and the zoo. 'Lots of things have happened beneath these windows,' she went on. 'The Russians camped over there at the end of the war,' she said pointing towards Heroes' Square. 'They ate the animals from the zoo when they had no food left. And of course in '56 the tanks came right down Dózsa György Street, here in front of us.' She lit a cigarette and took us into another large room. 'When my grandsons come they play table-tennis in here.' There was a full-size table-tennis table in the room, bats and ball on a nearby chair. She took us around the whole flat, but it was obvious that she only used the one room and the conservatory, unless she had family to stay.

On the other side of us lived another family, in what Marietta told us was a minuscule flat. We had not as yet seen them, but could often hear a child crying if we were in the bathroom.

This flat, unlike any of ours since Vántus Károly Street, had a telephone. The apparatus itself looked as though it belonged in a museum and it took a while to get accustomed to the complexities of using it. We were in fact 'sharing' a telephone with the family in the small flat next-door. This meant that when the phone rang it sounded in both households and whoever picked up the receiver first could hear the caller and the person in the other flat could hear nothing. If the call was for you then you continued the conversation. If the caller wanted the neighbour you simply replaced the receiver and the person next-door was put through. If you wanted to make a call it could happen that there was no line when you picked up the receiver. That meant the neighbour was using it and you would have to wait. But we were pleased at last to have a telephone at all.

It did not take too long before we got to know the couple next-door. Cili had worked in the pharmaceutical research institute but was now at home with her four-year-old daughter, Zsófi, and one-year-old son, Dani. Cili was vivacious and positive, down to earth and fun. She spoke some English and studied on her own when Dani had his nap. I was soon spending one or two lunchtimes there helping her towards the intermediate State English exam.

Cili and Laci's flat, all thirty-two square metres of it, was a perfect study in how to use space. Books lined all the walls of the room and the gallery which they had built. Toys were in boxes and boxes under tables, chairs and sofa pulled out into beds and a table pulled out from the wall, every cupboard door was covered with hooks and racks on the inside, and hooks came from high up on walls or from the ceiling to hang things on. It was comfortable and cosy, and although I could appreciate the difficulties of living in such cramped conditions I disliked leaving the intimacy of their flat for the aircraft-hangar dimensions of our own. Often I would hear the music of her favourite Bee-Gees through the bathroom wall and sometimes I would go over and have a coffee while Cili smoked and bustled about cooking and chatting. We were the same age but her experience, borne of two children, made me feel like her younger sister. She was looking forward to the birth of my baby, since Dani, she explained, was unfortunately already past the 'babying' stage.

It was towards the end of November that Paul's student Tamás offered to loan us a grand piano which one of his sisters had inherited, but which she had no room for in her present home. We accepted the offer gratefully, and thus it was that one evening Tamás, his brother (a priest), brother-in-law and two cousins turned up and heroically manhandled the instrument up to the first floor. It was badly out of tune, but useable, and I looked forward to Paul being able to accompany some of my cello pieces.

I was feeling well, but as winter approached I doubted if I would endure the long train journey to Germany. The snow came early and we decided to fly to Düsseldorf where my cousin would meet us and drive us north to Braunschweig. It was unusually cold in Germany too but as always the abundance of food, bright lights and good cheer created a warm atmosphere. Everyone was curious to know if we wanted a boy or a girl, and our standard response was to reply in union, Paul 'a boy' and myself 'a girl'. I was, in fact, indifferent, but partly as a reaction to a certain degree of Hungarian male chauvinism (when country people ask 'how many children do you have?' it traditionally means only the boys), I told everyone I wanted a daughter.

With the new year came the first of many falls of heavy snow. Roads were blocked, cars abandoned, and temperatures plummeted to minus twenty degrees. My cousin Ben was undaunted about driving us back to Düsseldorf, though we decided to leave a day early and stay the night in the house of another of my aunts who lived there. It was a painfully slow, tiring drive, with only one lane of the autobahn cleared in either direction and snow still falling thick and fast. I was sleepy and dozed on the back seat bundled up in blankets.

The flight from Düsseldorf to Munich was happily uneventful, but we had to leave the Lufthansa aircraft in

180

Munich where it was reported to be unfit to continue the journey. Sitting in the terminal we could see the de-icing machines working on every plane due to take off in the blizzard-like conditions.

We had to wait for ten hours before, at eight o'clock in the evening, a Malév, Hungarian airways, aircraft touched down on the snowy runway. We were soon aboard and took off into the night sky, though the snow obscured any view there might have been of the city below. The engines roared, the plane rattled and the 'fasten seat belts' sign continued to shine as the stewardesses walked up and down the steeply inclining aisle between the seats. It seemed as if we were struggling to maintain altitude throughout the flight, while the dim lights flickered and the windows froze up completely.

As we began our descent at Ferihegy airport the weather conditions appeared to be identical. It was disconcerting to be approaching an invisible runway, and after a surprisingly smooth landing the passengers burst into spontaneous applause of relief. The airport building was deserted, the luggage carousels at a standstill, and the few remaining staff obviously waiting to go home. We were told that the conditions in Budapest were catastrophic. No public transport was running except the underground, and no taxis back into town. We all huddled onto the two poorly-heated buses waiting outside and looked in silent disbelief at the mountains of snow on the roadside, the many abandoned cars and lorries, and listened to the silence of a city paralysed. We did not see another moving vehicle nor a single pedestrian in our long drive back. The buses drew up in Engels Square, where the drivers shrugged helplessly in reply to the requests for advice from those unlucky enough to live in Buda. We walked backwards against the raging wind towards the underground, dragging our suitcases along in the snow. We then repeated the procedure in a deserted Heroes' Square and along Dózsa György Street, until we were home.

Our flat was freezing cold having remained totally unheated for the two weeks of our absence. Unfortunately, the stove would take several days to warm up. The following morning the thermometer showed more than minus twenty while the silence of the empty streets in the pale sunshine was blissfully peaceful. I moved to the sofa but still cocooned myself in blankets, while Paul discovered that there had been no deliveries of bread or milk to our local shop and he had to go into the city centre to buy some food.

Cili popped in the same day, pleased to see us back. 'I've got the letter about my exam,' she said, 'it's at the end of the month.'

'Well, we can start today,' I replied.

She smiled. 'By the way, our telephone number's been changed,' she continued, telling me the new one. 'There's one problem though. The post office has given us the same number as the Hajdú washing machine repair shop, so every second call is from someone who wants their washing machine repaired.'

'Another service from the post office,' I muttered to myself.

I spent the afternoon ringing those people I could, to tell them of our new number. One of my calls was to Marina, my doctor, who was keen to see me. We arranged that I should go the following afternoon for a check-up. Public transport was still erratic so I decided to go by taxi. As we reached the centre of the town, however, I saw that all the traffic lights were switched off and a long queue of cars stretched in front of us. My taxi driver began to chat about the weather and the problems it had caused him, while I hoped I would still get to Marina on time. 'What's going on?' I asked him after some five minutes had passed.

'Oh, it's probably one of our friends or relatives,' he replied – referring to the politicians of neighbouring countries, 'they always come and go.' At that moment a cavalcade of shiny, black Mercedes cars bearing the red flag of the Soviet Union swept past, 'well, they don't *go* much,' he added meaningfully.

As we crossed Margaret Bridge I caught my breath again at the beauty of the view. The words of a Zorán song came to my mind, 'You know, *my* city has two parts.' And I thought, yes, this is my city now. I loved its hills, its dark backstreets and hidden restaurants, its smells, its courtyards, its trams.

Marina pronounced me to be in excellent health, as I in fact felt. She also did a scan which showed unequivocally that the child was a boy. Having thought of it as a girl for some months, I was glad to have time to readjust the picture of myself with a daughter to that of a son before the beginning of May when it, or rather *he*, was due.

The harsh winter continued and the Danube flowed slowly, a thick syrup with huge ice-flows like pieces of a giant jigsaw puzzle being carried downstream.

I continued with my private students and taught a few classes at the journalists' school to fill in for someone who was ill. It was always interesting to hear the stories behind the stories and to get advance information about political happenings. On one such visit I ran into the small tobacconist's opposite the journalist's school, hoping to be able to buy some coffee which had completely disappeared from the shops. I was, however, out of luck.

'So, where's all the coffee gone?' I demanded of my students when I got into the room.

'Don't worry,' one of them replied. 'It'll be back in the shops in the next few days. They're obviously going to put the price up, so they stop supplies for a bit so that everyone's desperate, then when it comes back into the shops people are so relieved that they don't complain whatever it costs.'

Cili and I were having one of our last practices for her oral exam when I had a surprise visit from Geoff. He had been conscripted into the army for a year the previous autumn, and very rarely got any time at home. He had been sent to Lenti, in the south-west of Hungary. We hugged each other then he stood back and looked at me, 'Good, now I can actually see you're pregnant,' he said.

'It's going to be a boy,' I replied.

'Well, couldn't you have him on my birthday, on the 5th?' he asked.

'I'll try,' I promised, smiling.

'I should be on leave for a few days then, what with May day,' he added.

I asked him what it was like in the army but he refused to be drawn, it was obviously something he wanted to forget for the short time he was away. The doorbell rang. It was Laurence. Geoff was as pleased to see him as I was. He walked straight into the sitting room peeling off layers of clothes and leaving small, melting puddles of snow where he stood. He made for a small table in the corner and automatically began to fiddle with the lamp next to the phone.

'So what have you been up to since we last saw you?' I asked him.

He shook his head with an exaggerated look of despair. 'Look at this,' he said, thrusting a small newspaper cutting into my hands. 'My mum seems to think I should go back to the Motherland and do a proper job.'

I began to laugh. 'But this is an advertisement for a trombonist in the BBC Symphony Orchestra!'

'Yes, I know,' he said, agitatedly pulling at the wire of the lamp. 'Anything that mentions music and she sends it; I don't even want to go back,' he said finally detaching the shade of the lamp from its base which went crashing to the floor. He placed the base next to the shade on the table and began to pace up and down. At that moment Paul arrived home with a four-hand version of Khatchaturian's ballet 'Gayaneh', and he and Laurence lost themselves in a frantic rendering of the 'Sabre Dance', while Geoff and I fell about laughing at their mad attempts to keep up the hysterical tempo.

It was at about this time that I finally allowed myself to be persuaded to make a visit to the British embassy to discuss the future nationality of my unborn baby. Various English people had told me that to assume he would automatically be granted British citizenship was folly. Thus, I approached one of the immaculately dressed women seated in the quiet, carpeted consular section of the embassy. Having requested an audience with the consul and filled in the appropriate forms, I was asked to wait. A few minutes later a grey-haired, bespectacled man in his late fifties appeared from behind one of the glass windows and called my name. It transpired after some ten minutes' questioning that my son could indeed have a British passport, but if he were to marry someone who was not British, their child – even if born in Britain – would have to apply for citizenship.

I considered a moment. 'Do you mean to say then, that there is no really good reason for me to travel to England to have this baby?' I asked him.

For a few seconds he said nothing. Then, leaning forwards in his seat and looking me straight in the eye over the rim of his glasses he said, 'Tell me – have you ever *been* in a Hungarian hospital?'

The winter snows melted and people began their annual look-out for the first signs of spring's approach. Danielle was due to visit at the end of March and would be giving a recital in the Austrian cultural attaché's residence.

Shortly before Danielle's arrival, at one of my check-ups with Marina, she told me that she would have to be in Armenia at the beginning of May. I was very disappointed. I trusted her and felt confident and relaxed about giving birth with her help. But as she pointed out, there was no possibility of Paul being present at the birth at her hospital. This was a new concept in Hungary, in fact Marina herself found the idea strange. She told me that she had already spoken to the consultant at the Railway Workers' Hospital, who had worked in England for four years, and he was willing to take me on as his patient. This was the only obstetrics department in the country where fathers could be present. I went to see him the following week. In the event he was friendly, spoke excellent English and reassured us that I was very healthy and he anticipated no problems, dismissing me with the words, 'Go away and enjoy yourself.'

I did. Danielle arrived and we spent our time going for walks, chatting in my favourite café, the Művész, and going to concerts and museums. And I sat lazily listening to her play through her recital programme at the Austrian cultural attaché's residence, with the windows open to the warm spring breeze and the birdsong outside.

Attila rang and invited us all to go on a horse and cart ride in the countryside just on the outskirts of Budapest. He was planning to take groups of German tourists for an authentic Hungarian *gulyás* to be cooked in the middle of the fields and woods, and was now ready to do a dry run before taking his first group. I could imagine no more pleasant way of spending a warm spring afternoon than being gently jogged along on a horse-drawn cart, but both Paul and Danielle were against it. 'I don't think you'd better come,' said Danielle, 'What happens if you go into labour or something?'

'Oh, come off it!' I protested, 'I'm fine, nothing will happen!'

But Paul shook his head. 'No, we can all stay at home if you don't want to feel left out, but you're not going on any horse ride.'

I did not at all mind staying at home alone, but I would have liked the cart ride. 'No, you go, it'll be fun; I'll do some cello practice, I haven't done any for ages.'

It was arranged for the following morning and Attila assured me that Paul and Danielle would be back at four or five o'clock in the afternoon. As it happened I spent a lazy day because Cili, who bumped into Paul and Danielle on their way out, insisted I go and have lunch with her, and that included the remainder of the afternoon. Laci came back from work at around five and I went back home to get the meal ready for Paul and Danielle.

The hours passed – seven, eight o'clock and no sign. The phone rang. It was Attila's wife Anna, to say that there had been a delay and they would be home soon, but she was either unwilling or unable to give me any further details.

At a quarter to nine I heard the front door open. I walked out of the sitting-room into the hall. 'So what happened?' I asked. Danielle groaned, leaning against the wall with her eyes closed. I turned to Paul. 'Well?' Paul opened his mouth as though to speak, but hysterical laughter took its place. He could hardly stand, tears of mirth ran down his cheeks as he staggered into the room. Danielle had not moved. 'Tell me what happened!' I said, starting to laugh myself. It took a long time before Paul was able to speak comprehensibly.

The trip had started well. There were in fact two carts, the one they had travelled in being covered like a wagon and packed with food, drink and cooking utensils. The horses were a bit frisky, but Paul said that the first part of the trip was uneventful. The carts made their way along the village street to the edge of the wood where an unmade track led down through the trees. The rain of the previous week had dried, leaving deep ruts in the mud where other carts had passed through. A few other people had joined the outing and were travelling in the first, open cart, Paul and Danielle behind. Their wagon was forced to make a short, unscheduled stop when one of the horses' feeding buckets fell off. The other cart slowly continued down to the bottom of the path and out of sight around a corner and into an open field. Having remounted, the driver hurried the horses along to catch up with the others. It was at this point that things began to get out of control. The horses were, it seemed, just waiting for this kind of encouragement, and thoroughly bored with their unaccustomed load to pull, took off at speed down the track. The cart wheels were caught in the ruts, and try as he might, the driver was completely unable to slow the animals down. As they hurtled in a cloud of dust towards the sharp bend at the bottom of the hill, the horses parted company from the cart. They successfully negotiated the turn, but the cart was flung over to one side, catapulting unsuspecting passengers and the food over the hedge and into the neighbouring field. Bruised, dazed and breathless, Paul and Danielle found themselves sitting among a heap of cooking pans, onions and broken eggs, the cart in the hedge, and the horses nowhere to be seen.

Danielle, never having been designed for anything more athletic than a short run to catch a bus, gingerly picked herself up and dusted herself down. Having reassured herself that she had not sustained any permanent injuries, she began to look for her handbag and glasses on the ground. The others came running back along the track and managed to right the cart, their driver had already caught the two runaway horses. Attila was full of apologies. No, these horses had never actually pulled a cart before but they were usually reliable. Danielle was not amused. She was as yet unconvinced that she would be able to give her recital two days later.

Attila decided that they should go ahead with the cooking and Paul sat, bursting into laughter every few minutes as he gazed at a dazed and dishevelled Danielle and recalled their dramatic flight into the field.

The *gulyás* was duly cooked and eaten, the horses once more tethered to the carts and the convoy moved off. The carts emerged from the fields and woods out onto the road near the bottom of the hill leading back up into the village. But the horses were playing up again. Danielle prepared to abandon the cart and walk, but the driver persuaded her that everything would be alright. Yet no matter how he cracked his whip, they steadfastly refused to go up the hill. Then, making a sudden decision, the driver turned the cart around, shouting at the horses, and galloped them down the hill. In the middle of the road was a small green with bushes. They shot around it at top speed so that before the horses realised what was happening they were heading back up the hill. The sheer velocity at which they were travelling lifted Danielle off her wooden seat. With one hand she clutched at her glasses, with the other she grasped the seat, and lacking a third she watched helplessly as her handbag bounced to the back of the cart. She was too shocked to utter a sound as they hurtled through the village, before coming to an abrupt standstill further on.

It was not until the following morning that she felt up to speaking on the subject, and it was days before Paul could stop himself laughing at odd moments whenever he looked at Danielle. And I was forced to admit what a good thing it was I had agreed to stay at home.

★ ★ ★ ★ ★

As April came and went I had to go for more regular check-ups at the hospital. I was lucky, the Railway Workers' Hospital was on the same block where we lived. The baby was due on the 2nd of May, and on the 1st I had a phone call from Geoff. He was going to the Mayday parade and wanted to know if I was interested in going too. We joined the seething mass of people carrying balloons and flags and headed for the middle of the park where hundreds of stalls sold everything from leather belts to pancakes and from silver jewelry to bars of chocolate. 'Don't do that!' Geoff shouted at me as I jumped down from a low wall onto the path by the lake, 'You're not to have him for another four days yet!'

The next day I had another quick check-up and then I went off to hear an English pianist friend give a recital. I felt relaxed and happy. The following two days dragged by – I had not planned anything and now I just wanted to have the baby. I had partly packed my bag, but without any urgency.

'There's no need to rush at the first sign,' my doctor had said, 'a first birth is usually ten hours or so, and you live next-door.'

It was May 5th, so it did not look as though I could keep my promise to Geoff after all. We went to bed at eleven o'clock, I tossed and turned as usual, looking forward to when I would once again be able to fall asleep on my stomach.

Shortly after midnight I awoke to find the bed swimming with water. I got up, startled. I sat on a chair. Was this it? How could it be that I felt no contractions? I woke Paul. He jumped out of bed and began pulling on his clothes. 'Let's go!' he said.

'But I can't feel anything, I don't think we need to rush.'

He sat back down on the bed. 'Do you think there's time for me to make a pot of tea?' he asked hopefully.

'Why not?' I answered.

Paul made the tea and brought it into the bedroom on a tray. We sat and chatted while Paul found the book on childbirth he had promised the doctor to read as a condition of being allowed to attend the birth. But before he could look up the relevant passage I felt a strong squeeze which took my breath away. Another followed quickly. 'Shall we go now?' Paul asked noticing my change of demeanour.

'I don't think I can walk,' I gasped. I glanced at the clock, almost one o'clock.

'I'll get a taxi.'

I smiled. I wondered what the driver's reaction would be to driving me just around the block.

Paul ran along Dózsa György Street to the taxi rank on Heroes' Square. 'Learn Hungarian' had not prepared him for this particular turn of events. There was only one car there, its driver snoozing peacefully. Paul ran up and knocked on the window. 'Szülés van! Szülés van' 'There's a birth!' he yelled dramatically.

The poor driver, as if awaking to a dream called, 'Hol? Hol?' 'Where? Where?'

Paul explained and they drove the few yards back along Dózsa György Street to our house.

I had managed to throw a few more things into my bag and was half-dressed. Paul helped me with my socks and shoes and we headed for the front door. A light shone from around Cili's doorway and a moment later she appeared in a dressing gown. 'Good luck!' she said as we walked slowly down the stairs, 'I won't be able to get to sleep now!'

The taxi driver took us around the corner to the side entrance of the hospital. 'All the best!' he said patting Paul on the shoulder. I felt alright as long as I stood still during a contraction. We made our way up the dimly-lit stone steps to the first floor, and knocked on the door. I handed my papers over to the nurse.

'What has happened so far?' she asked me.

'The waters broke at midnight,' I replied.

She took a sheet of paper and put it into an ancient typewriter. Glancing at the clock I saw it was one twenty. 'Alright, put these on,' she said, handing me a white nightdress-like garment. Another nurse came in and examined me. She took my notes and then said, 'When did the waters break?'

'At midnight.'

'And you felt nothing before that?'

'I was asleep,' I said.

'Well, we'll be lucky if the doctor gets here before this baby is born,' she said. 'Is your husband staying?'

'Yes,' I replied.

She picked up the phone and rang my doctor. 'Okay, come this way,' she said to us both.

As we approached the labour rooms I heard frantic scream-ing and doctors' voices urging calm and more pushing. 'Good God,' I thought, 'this is really it.' I was taken into the room next-door but soon became oblivious of the tortured screams as I fought to concentrate on the breathing exercises I had practised, and I watched the two nurses going in turn to the window to see if my doctor was coming. After that, time stood still. Later, I had vague memories of seeing the doctor's face smiling as he came into the room, apparently at two o'clock, and before half past two John was there, a screaming bundle of red and pink.

As I lay, tired and unbelieving I heard Paul say, 'Well, that's not what they said in the book!'

The doctor laughed. 'I'll come and see you later this morning, you try and get some sleep.'

Paul stayed a while and after he had gone I was wheeled to the ward. The other five inmates were asleep, it was dawn. I was put in the bed next to the windows. There was a door leading out onto the long verandah which looked out over a large yard full of trees, on the other side of which stood our house. The sun was just coming up orange and pink through the branches, and the birds were singing loudly, ecstatically, as I surely felt they should.

My five days in hospital were thankfully uneventful. The food was inedible and in anticipation of this I had taken a large bag of muesli – I made it myself, since it was generally possible to obtain the ingredients, but no-one had heard of muesli itself. I soon became rather self-conscious about eating it however, as patients and nurses alike crowded round to watch.

'What's it got in it?' asked one nurse.

'Oats..' I began.

'Oats!' she exclaimed. 'But that's what horses eat!'

Visiting times were strictly limited but Cili, in her white pharmacist's coat, came and went whenever she felt like it. It was strange to have to take and wash up our own cutlery, but even the other women seemed surprised when a nurse put her head through the door saying, 'Who wants clean sheets?' We all put up our hands. She counted out the requisite number, dropped them onto a chair and walked on to the next ward leaving us to do the rest ourselves.

The babies were beautifully cared for and were delivered, at every feeding time, on the double-decker trolley, with neatly arranged hair and spotless clothes. Apart from a touch of jaundice John was faring well and was already putting on weight before we left the hospital.

Back home life lost the calm and order of hospital routine. John proved to be the sort of nightmare new-born one reads of in baby books, the ones who are either dropped out of fifth-floor windows or whose mothers take the plunge instead. He slept neither night or day for more than twenty

192

minutes at a time. Tamás sent round his brother Guszti, a hospital paediatrician to see us. He was very quiet-mannered, calm, reassuring: John was perfectly healthy, putting on a large amount of weight, but some babies, he explained, – especially boys – were like that. He suggested that if our nerves could stand it we should leave him to cry. It was not often that I could bear to listen to it, but the way of taking my mind off the awful noise was to read, and what I decided to tackle was my first venture into Hungarian literature: Örkény's One-Minute Short Stories. These were what filled the dark, sleepless nights, not just the minutes but the hours too, for many months.

Hardly had we begun to adjust to life as a family when we were packing up to leave for a summer in England. We had agreed with Ági and Kazi that they would have the flat in July and August, and so we had booked our flight for the end of June. Our Hungarian friends were, for the most part, shocked not to say horrified. 'You're taking a six-week old on an aeroplane?' they asked. In vain I tried to explain that it was no different from going on a bus or in a car.

There were absolutely no baby-changing facilities at the airport, but two cooing stewardesses led me into an area of aeroplane seats in a room which was used for staff-training, and I was able to change him there.

The customs official abandoned his routine questions about Hungarian currency and what we had in our suitcases. 'How old is the baby now?' he asked me. I told him. 'So when did he last feed? And are you going to feed him on the plane? Is he going to see his grandparents?' Other passengers waited patiently until he had satisfied himself that John would survive the journey ahead.

It was a difficult few weeks travelling the length and breadth of England with a baby that hardly slept and cried all night. We returned to Hungary in the first days of September to a phone call offering us some English language-recordings at Hungaroton at a very high fee. The only difficulty would be that they were at night, from ten o'clock until two or three in the morning and so we would need a baby-sitter. Tamás suggested his younger sister who had had plenty of experience with her countless nephews and nieces. I warned her of the difficulties of an incessantly crying infant, but she was unperturbed.

There were only four of us involved in the recording, one of the others being Laurence. Inevitably someone began to doze off somewhere after midnight, and our rumbling stomachs were recorded by the sensitive microphones. However, we managed to finish in four nights instead of the five allotted, and the recording hardly revealed our somnambulent state.

Although we did not realise it then, this was to be our last job with Laurence. Not many days later he disappeared off to London for an interview with Andrew Lloyd-Webber's company for the position of musical director. He was finally offered the job at the age of just twenty three. On the morning of his departure, we had a frantic phone call. 'Paul can you get down here to Keleti straight away? I had to pay my train ticket in hard currency and I've got absolutely nothing left – can you lend me some?' Paul found twenty pounds and ran to get a bus. As I watched him go from the window I found it difficult to imagine that Laurence would no longer be coming round to play excerpts from his latest compositions on our still out-of-tune piano, share a bowl of pasta with us or complain passionately about some ludicrous piece of local bureaucracy. We would miss him greatly.

Late in September, Miklós called in to see me. He was very excited about a meeting he had been to outside Budapest in a place called Lakitelek, at which a new political party was being formed. 'I know you're not interested in politics,' he said,' but really important things are happening now. You can't live in this part of the world and be as indifferent to politics as you westerners are.'

'Alright, alright,' I demurred, acknowledging the truth of his observation.

He went on to tell me that he was thinking of applying for a scholarship to spend a year in America, though he would probably not go until the following September.

The autumn passed quickly. The last stray tourists disappeared, the fur hats and black leather coats came out of mothballs as the days became short and dark. This was our first Christmas in Hungary which meant we would have to send all our presents by post to relatives in both Germany and England. John was now too heavy for the sling I had been carrying him in, so I transported him in a backpack. This was also a cause of mild sensation and elicited some concerned questioning from older women on public transport. John himself was quite happy, able to see everything around him as we did our Christmas shopping. The main streets and small squares were lined with covered stalls selling handicraft items. Vapours of hot, mulled wine permeated the cold December air and coloured light-bulbs strung between the booths lent an atmosphere of gaiety to the otherwise dimly-lit city. It was from these stalls that I chose my presents, knowing that their unusualness would be much appreciated.

When I had packed my parcels I left John with Paul for the morning and headed for the post office at Nyugati station. Redirected from the main entrance to one at the side of the building, I found myself in a crush of men and women all weighed down with brown paper packages. I had already been told by Cili that you were not permitted to use sellotape, at least it should not be visible, because the customs officials opened all parcels. The technique was somehow to put the tape under the brown paper. I could see various people around me filling in forms, but these, of course, had to be asked for.

After about twenty minutes I reached the counter. The man weighed each parcel and gave me the customs declaration forms. Then, picking up the smallest of the three parcels he said, 'You can't send this one, it's got no string on it, all parcels have to have string. And anyway, this can go letter post, take it to the main part of the post office.'

'Do you have any string here, or can I buy some in the post office?' I asked.

He shook his head. I filled in all three forms and queued again to give in my two larger parcels. More than forty minutes after entering the post office I was back out on the street.

I managed to buy some string and I also bought some silver baking foil, remembering that Caroline had told me it was unavailable before Christmas, since the whole amount produced was used to wrap the chocolate fondants traditionally hung on Hungarians' Christmas trees.

I made my way back to the main part of the post office and found a small shelf where I could tie up the parcel. It was then I realised I had no scissors. Try as I might, I could not bite or chew through the string, but a woman watching my antics offered me her nail file. I now looked at the long queues stretching from every window – I would be there till lunchtime. A pall of unseasonal gloom hung over the whole place, the silence broken only by the squeak and clatter of the swing doors, the banging of rubber stamps and the sighs of those standing in line. Finally it was my turn. The unsmiling woman, without so much as glancing at me, pushed the parcel back. 'You can't send this,' she said, 'the value of the contents you have written on here exceeds the limit.'

'What is the limit?' I asked.

'Eight hundred forints, you'll have to send the things in two parcels.'

The person behind me was already pushing their letters under the glass as I stood wondering what to do next. There was no way I was going home to repack the parcel into two. I walked back around to the parcels' office and brazenly went to the front of the queue to ask for another form. Then out onto the side street and into the main entrance where I was careful to join a different queue, my form now stating that the parcel was worth five hundred forints. Once again I found myself at the front. I said a silent prayer. But in vain.

The woman pushed my parcel back towards me. 'You can't send chocolates out of the country,' she said, pointing to where I had written the word 'chocolate' on my form.

Without a word I picked up my parcel and walked away. I joined a third queue, taking a pen out of my bag and obliterating the offending word on the green paper. I decided that if the customs wanted to remove the chocolates from the parcel they were welcome to do so, but I would not. This time I succeeded in disposing of my parcel, and I fled the building vowing to investigate any and every alternative for sending presents abroad before the following Christmas.

On the corner near our house I decided to buy one or two things at the greengrocer's. This was a private premises, it could not be described as a shop, merely a makeshift construction, but it had good-quality produce. There was no-one else there, and having weighed my apples, the greengrocer looked around, lowered his voice and said, 'Do you want some bananas?' I had not seen a banana since our summer in England. I nodded. Surreptitiously, and with a conspiratorial look I imagined would more usually accompany the supply of pornographic material, he pulled a box out from under the counter. 'You can have up to three kilos,' he whispered. I took the three offered, deciding to give some to Cili and maybe to one or two other friends. They were quickly concealed in a large, brown paper bag. 'Don't tell anyone where you got them,' he said under his breath, as he handed them over.

In the week before Christmas the same greengrocer was selling pine trees and we bought ours there. On the evening of the 23rd, decorating the tree, we became aware of singing somewhere close by. We looked at each other wonderingly, then walked to our front door. Outside, on the stairway, stood Tamás with about a dozen members of his church choir. They did not stop singing as we walked out to greet them, and several other residents of the building were now standing in their doorways to listen. When they finished that particular carol they came in, all wishing us a happy Christmas.

'Well, this is your first Christmas in Hungary,' said Tamás, 'and as you have no family here and you're on your own, we thought we'd come and sing to you.'

They sang several more carols after which we all drank mulled wine and they left to sing to one or two other deserving people. John cried all night on the 24th, we slept no more than about twenty minutes in all, and sitting down to dinner on the 25th I looked like Dickens' Ghost of Christmas Past.

New year 1988 began with some political surprises. For the first time the idea of tax was introduced, both VAT and income tax.

Paul immediately saw the writing on the wall. 'No taxation without representation,' he predicted. I was doubtful that any major changes could possibly take place, but he was adamant. 'You don't think people are going to pay tax to a government they didn't vote for, and when they have no say about where the money's going?'

I did not know. Aside from the fact that day-to-day politics did not particularly interest me, we had had no television since 1983 and I had neither the time nor the patience to struggle with a newspaper. Developments which affected everyone's daily lives were usually imparted to me by friends or students.

In February a photographer friend of ours, Imi, called in to see us. He lived in the next street and had taken photos of John as a small baby, and for Christmas to send to friends and relatives. He was planning to drive to the town of Mohács in the south of the country to take photographs of the annual busójárás or carnival to mark the winter solstice. We had seen pictures of people dressed in strange costumes with grotesque masks, but had never been to the event itself. Paul suggested I go and that he would have John for the day.

We left early in the morning, driving along deserted country roads between white, frosted fields. We went first to Baja, where Miklós had been teaching, and picked him up from the newly-built hotel on Petőfi Island. In Mohács we parked the car and followed the ambling droves of people up the main street. In the town square was a huge bonfire, its sparks rising up against the pale blue, wintry sky. Standing nearby were figures in long, fleecy garments with masks of red and orange, leering menacingly. Some of them chased passers-by, pelting them with flour from small bags hanging by their sides. Sitting to one side of the fire was a gypsy who had removed his mask and who looked decidedly drunk. A moment later a friend of his turned up, and pushing his mask on top of his head, accepted the proffered bottle.

'I'm going to take some pictures,' said Imi.

'What, of them?' I asked, nodding towards the gypsies, 'they may not be very happy about that.'

'All you have to do is talk to the people you want to photograph first, you don't show them the camera till later, it's not a problem,' Imi replied, strolling off in their direction. We watched from a distance. Imi began talking to the two men, accepted a swig from the bottle and sat down next to them.

Miklós and I walked on up the main street, trying to avoid being showered with flour. Sitting on one or two benches were people selling the kind of masks the men were wearing. Each was different, hand carved, most made of wood with two horns and a fleecy mop of hair on top. We both considered buying one to take home and put on the wall, but could not find one we really liked. Slowly, we made our way back to the fire just in time to see Imi taking his last photos of his new-found friends, posing happily. It was lunchtime and we decided to find a restaurant. We took a turning down a narrow side street which wound among the small houses. Quite suddenly something caught my eye – a mask, with a For Sale sign next to it, was hanging in the window of a house.

Miklós followed my gaze. 'You want to buy it?' he asked me.

'I'm not sure,' I replied, 'Let's go and have lunch and I'll decide.' We found a local restaurant nearby where both

Miklós and Imi expounded on the superior quality, not to say quantity, of food in country restaurants.

As we paid to leave Miklós asked me, 'Have you made up your mind about the mask then?'

I nodded, 'Yes, I'll get it, it's much better than those we saw up in the town.' But as we approached the house we could see the mask had disappeared. 'I should have bought it when I saw it,' I said.

'Let's go and ask if they've got another one,' Miklós suggested.

'If they had, they'd have put it in the window, wouldn't they?' I replied, disappointedly walking on.

Miklós shook his head at me and approached the front door, while Imi and I stood at a distance. A middle-aged woman greeted him.

'Do you have any more masks for sale?' asked Miklós, 'My friend wanted to buy the one that was there an hour ago,' he continued, nodding towards me.

The woman smiled, hesitated a moment and then said, 'Please come in.' Imi and I walked over and followed Miklós into the house. We were led into a small, neat sitting room and asked to sit down. She disappeared for a moment, returning with a plate of doughnuts she had just made. 'Help yourselves,' she invited, sitting down next to us. 'That mask was made by my son,' she began, 'he makes them for exhibitions, he was apprenticed to a really well-known craftsman, but he doesn't usually sell them,' she said. 'But he's getting married soon and they need money for furniture so he decided to sell just one or two. I haven't got any more here, but if you really want one I could take you around to his flat – I can't promise you anything though.'

Miklós raised his eyebrows at me, questioningly. I nodded, smiling.

The woman led us through narrow streets of old houses to where two new blocks of flats stood. We walked up to the first floor where she knocked on one of the doors. 'It's me,' she called. The door opened. The woman explained the situation to the young man in the doorway, who then stood aside to let us in.

The flat was identical to the prefabricated concrete blocks to be found all over the country, but the hall was made unique by the masks which covered every inch of space on its walls. Pointing to a part of the wall between the front door and the kitchen he said, 'You can choose one of these, the others are not for sale. I exhibit them,' he went on, lifting a mask down to show us the paper glued to the back of it stating the place and date of where it had last been exhibited. 'They're not like the ones you saw in the town today – these are not painted, I stain them with pigs' blood. And these are real cow's horns and sheep's wool.' Like the mask I eventually chose, most were black with leering smiles showing all their teeth, and with menacing eyes peering out from behind their shaggy manes. He explained that it was a real wrench for him to part with any of them.

Later, as we left, saying goodbye to mother and son, Miklós looked at my happy smile as I examined the mask. 'You see?' he said, 'What would you do without me?'

★ ★ ★ ★ ★

Spring arrived in March in time for the celebrations on the 15th. It was always a rather tense time, since the uprising of the Hungarians against the Austrians was a purely national event, in no way connected with the Russians or socialism. Yet everywhere the red flag hung alongside the Hungarian tricolour. Nowhere was it more hated than by the statue of Sándor Petőfi, the poet famed to have inspired the revolution, where small Hungarian and red flags on sticks were put in the flower beds around the statue on the Danube bank. In fact, my first group of students from the Economics University had told me that they went at night and removed the red flags. It was a risky business with police with cameras all around the area. This year several thousand people openly protested in Petőfi Square for democracy and freedom. Two years previously a smaller such demonstration had been broken up by the police, but this time they remained simple bystanders. It certainly felt as though momentum was building towards some kind of political change.

As the spring went on we began to consider our plans for the summer. Neither of us could summon up much enthusiasm for another safari to England. However, it would not be possible to stay in the flat since Ági and Kazi would be using it in July and August. Luckily, a solution soon presented itself: I had returned to teaching the children who had been to school in Libya, and one of the families – whose three daughters were among my pupils – were going to Greece for the month of July. They suggested we go and house-sit for them, water the plants and take care of their dog.

Meanwhile, we could not but become aware of an undercurrent of excitement, a buzz in the air, as one previously unimaginable political change was followed by another. More new parties were being formed, while the ruling socialist party was shedding its hard-liners. On June 16th came the most provocative demonstration thus far, when people gathered at a plot in the cemetery where Imre Nagy was buried. Imre Nagy was Prime Minister in October 1956, prior to the revolution, and had declared Hungary's neutrality and its intention of withdrawing from the Warsaw Pact. When the Russians invaded at the beginning of November, Nagy sought refuge in the Yugoslav embassy. Later in the same month, having received personal assurances of his safety, Nagy left the embassy. He was arrested by the Russians, taken to Romania and in 1957 was returned to prison in Budapest. After several trials held in 1958 Nagy was executed on June 16th. This demonstration at the cemetery was broken up by the police. And yet the atmosphere of liberalisation persisted, stimulating a sense of freedom of expression among ordinary people.

It was this feeling that led to a far larger demonstration only some ten days later, to express people's outrage at what was happening across the border in Romania. The territory of Transylvania, formerly Hungarian, is home to some two million Hungarians, and the Ceausescu government had decided to bulldoze villages in the area and re-house those from their communities in concrete housing estates. Thus, on the evening of June 27th, I stood at the window from where I could see down Dózsa György Street and to Heroes' Square. Thousands of torch-bearing Hungarians marched into the square to demonstrate solidarity with their Transylvanian compatriots, a direct challenge to the government to take some positive action to prevent what was perceived as a deliberate attempt to further weaken the position of ethnic Hungarians. A gathering of such magnitude could not be suppressed without adverse publicity in the western press, and it passed off unchallenged.

At the beginning of July we moved out to where we were to house-sit on the very edge of Buda. In fact, on the city map the road was the last in that direction. To describe it as a road would be an exaggeration as it was no more than some steep steps leading down a hillside beyond which lay a deeply-wooded valley. We had visited Marcsi and Gyula a few days prior to their departure for Greece to learn the ins and outs of locking up, the dog-feeding routine and the plants to be watered. We did not plan to go anywhere or do anything in particular – it was extremely hot and a great relief to be out of the stifling city. In addition, I had just had the fact confirmed that I was pregnant, and I felt like sleeping at every available opportunity. It was during the peaceful days we spent here that I first conceived of the idea of writing a book, though I was unsure how to set about organising all the memories and impressions of the previous years.

Our plan had been to stay in the house for the entire month of July, but this proved impossible. Emerging from the bathroom one evening Paul said, 'I think there's something wrong with the plumbing – I can hear the sound of rushing water from behind the bathroom wall, it could be a burst pipe.'

203

'Does it matter much?' I asked in my usual impractical way.

Paul looked heavenwards. 'The whole wall could come down – just go and listen, it sounds like a waterfall. I'll have to find the mains tap,' and so saying he disappeared out of the kitchen door and outside.

I walked into the bathroom. It was exactly as he had described. However, in the dark outside, our search to locate the tap proved fruitless. 'Why don't we try the neighbours, maybe they can help?' I suggested.

Paul walked up the few steps as far as the gate of the nearest house. He returned alone a few minutes later. 'Let's say they weren't very enthusiastic about the idea,' he told me.

'You mean they wouldn't even come and look?' I asked in surprise.

Paul shook his head. This was not a response we had encountered from neighbours in any of the five flats we had thus far rented, and it seemed to me that attitudes more prevalent in the west of keeping oneself to oneself, and leaving others to their own troubles, had reached the more affluent corners of Hungary too. We walked back into the house and debated what to do next.

'Why don't we try Tamás?' I said, having discounted a whole list of friends who either had no phone or were on holiday. "He knows so many people, maybe he can give us the telephone number of a plumber.'

Paul reached into the basket with coins for the phone and headed back outside. He returned after some minutes saying that Tamás had asked him to ring back half an hour later, by which time he hoped to have contacted someone who could help us. When Paul rang again it transpired that Tamás had enlisted the help of two of his cousins, one of whom – Laci – had attended some of Paul's English lessons at the Music Academy. They arrived half an hour later, and as it turned out, switching off the water proved far simpler than finding their way to the house. Paul's suspicions were confirmed.

There was indeed a burst pipe, and the only immediate course of action was to switch the water off at the mains. Inevitably, this meant we would have to leave. Laci told us not to worry, that among the many members of his and Tamás's families someone would find us somewhere to go. He arranged to meet Paul the following day in the Music Academy library.

Paul went while John and I spent most of the day on the shady terrace outside the kitchen, playing with the dog and trying to entice the family of cats down from the steep embankment that rose up behind the house.

It was very peaceful there, the only sound was the wind as it rustled through the swaying sea of trees all around. The balmy nights were filled with the sound of crickets, like the backdrop to a film about Africa, and if I climbed to the top of the steps beside the house I could see the city spread out before me, the dark plain of Pest, and the even darker hills of Buda, a million lights twinkling far below; and in the distance there was always the lone barking of a dog, somewhere further down the hillside, unable to disturb the deep peace of the sleeping gardens and the still deeper silence of the wooded valley.

When Paul returned from the Academy, it was with some unexpected news. He had met Laci as arranged, but while they were considering the various options of where we could go, they were overheard by someone who had come to return a book to the library. This was János, the conductor of the Tomkins choir who sang, among other things, English madrigals. Paul had often helped them with their pronunciation, prior to a concert. On learning the gist of the situation János immediately insisted that we go and stay in his flat, since he was travelling to Lake Balaton the next day with his wife and three children, and they would be away for a month. We contacted Marcsi's parents and related the situation to them, and they agreed to come and water the plants and feed the dog.

So we moved back into the heart of the city, into the very street in which the Music Academy stands. The flat was huge, larger than any I had so far been in, though it was stiflingly hot. I went out early in the morning to do the shopping, we ate salads and fruit to avoid standing over a hot stove, and only in the evening did we venture out to the city park with John to stroll around the lake and feed the ducks.

One evening as we were preparing to leave, there was a ring at the door. I heard Paul shout in enthusiastic surprise as he saw who was there – Laurence. 'At last I've found you!' he said, walking in. 'I've been to Ági and Kazi's who told me you were in the wilds of Buda somewhere. I found my way halfway there, but then I had to get a taxi and even he had no idea where he was going. And once I'd found the house an old lady watering the flowers in the garden told me you were here!' Paul took Laurence into the sitting room while I went down into Liszt Ferenc Square with John to buy some ice-cream from the cake shop. When we got back, and as I put my key in the lock, I could hear music. Laurence was seated at the grand piano which dominated the sitting-room, illustrating something to Paul, who was seated close-by. They stopped to eat the ice-cream, after which Laurence helped bath John and put him to bed. We then resumed our seats around the piano while he entertained us with stories about his new life in London working for Andrew Lloyd Webber. This was what had brought him to Budapest. He was now responsible for travelling to cities where any Lloyd Webber productions were being performed, and ascertaining their quality. If he was unsatisfied, he was supposed to take rehearsals to improve the standard. In Budapest he had come to watch the production of 'Cats' which he had found perfectly satisfactory.

We saw Laurence several more times during his short stay, and together we trekked out to a remote part of Buda where Margó and István, with whom we had all travelled to England two years previously, had just bought a plot of land and were laying the foundations for a new house.

The days passed, hot and still, the city shrouded in a heat haze you could see if you were up in the hills. Tamás's cousin

Laci had called in to say that if we had nowhere to go for the last part of August, we were welcome to stay with himself and his new wife Rita, in the village of Sárisáp, some twenty miles outside Budapest where Rita was the doctor at the local agricultural co-operative. We welcomed an opportunity to escape the oppressive city heat, and in the evening of the day that János returned from Lake Balaton, we were driven out to Sárisáp. Village life was quiet and uneventful, and we passed the week sitting lazily in the garden, playing with John, and reading. The only surprising thing we learnt about Sárisáp was that there was no refuse collection, and that the local people dumped all their rubbish on a tip alongside the main road out of the village.

We knew Ági and Kazi were returning to Brussels before the end of the month, in good time for the new school term, so at the end of August, with already a tinge of autumn mist in the air, we returned to Budapest.

And though all Hungarians, like us, had abandoned their capital city for July and August, they were now refreshed to resume life where they had left off in June, but September began with another demonstration. This time it was against the building of a huge hydroelectric dam on the Danube which, it was said, would do great environmental damage. It was also in September that large numbers of Hungarians who had been executed in the aftermath of the '56 revolution (along with Imre Nagy) were rehabilitated.

Late in September Paul resumed working at the Academy. I began to teach the two children's groups once again, and to mark translations for the state language examination centre. I had been back to my doctor at the Railway Workers' Hospital and told I was fit and well. Marina also wanted to keep an eye on me, and after doing a scan, she told me that the baby was probably a girl.

As autumn passed into winter rumours began predicting price-rises which would double or treble the cost of goods. Wild speculation grew out of a more general consensus that

1989 would mark a dramatic change in Hungary's politics and economy. I was, however, totally unprepared for what I saw. In an unprecedented spending spree people were buying two and three televisions, fridges, hi-fis, merely to put their savings into a commodity they could sell in the new year. Shops became a wasteland of empty shelves and denuded stockrooms. On December 30th I went to the Lehel Square market where I had shopped almost daily in our Szinyei Street days. As I stepped off the tram and walked into the area of the huge market place, all I could see were small clusters of stall-holders, deeply engrossed in conversation, their completely stripped stalls behind them. I looked about me in sheer amazement – there was no food of any description anywhere.

In January new laws were passed on the right of assembly and the formation of new political parties and there could be no doubt as to where all this was leading.

By February our thoughts were more focused on the imminent birth of our second child. She – if indeed it was to be a girl – was due on the 13th and I somehow hoped it might be the 14th, St. Valentine's day. We had arranged with Cili next-door that she would take care of John when Paul went into the hospital with me. The 14th came and went, and the following day I had to go for a check-up.

'Absolutely no sign of this baby being born yet,' my doctor pronounced, 'It could be another week or two. Come back the day after tomorrow and I'll see you again.'

I was in no particular hurry, especially now that John – and we – were at last sleeping through most nights, and I knew that the baby would put an end to that.

Late in the evening I was marking work and Paul listening to some music on the radio when I began to feel an aching in my back and a general sensation of discomfort. It was eleven o'clock, so I decided to have a warm bath and go to sleep. As I got into bed Paul came in to get something from his desk.

'Well, who knows, tomorrow may be the day,' he said.

'Could well be,' I answered, 'I feel a bit odd.'

What do you mean? Shouldn't we go to the hospital?' asked Paul in more urgent tones.

'No chance,' I replied turning over, 'I want a good night's sleep.'

'Oh, no you don't!' he retorted. 'John's birth wasn't exactly textbook, you might easily have had him at home, and second babies are usually quicker. No, we're going, even if they just send us home again – I'm not delivering it here!'

'Don't worry, Cili would know what to do,' I said yawning and lazily pulling up the covers.

But it was too late. Panic had set in and Paul was already on his way to ask Cili to come and sleep in our flat to look after John. I groaned and got out of bed. Paul arrived back with Cili who looked suitably excited.

'Have you had any contractions?' she asked.

'No,' I replied, 'but my back aches. You really needn't stay, I'm sure they'll send me home again.'

I got dressed, and together we walked around the block to the hospital entrance. The night duty doctor was duly awoken and summoned, and I was taken off to be examined.

'The cervix is six centimetres open,' he said, 'you'll have to stay here.'

'But I'm not having any contractions, surely I can go home for tonight, I only live on the corner.' I was persuaded to remain in the labour room while the nurse promised to ring him if anything happened. It was a long night. Women came, had their babies, and went. Every hour or so a nurse came and attached me to a machine designed to monitor contractions, but the result was the same – nothing. I felt exhausted.

Some time before eight o'clock the following morning my doctor arrived. Having seen me less then twenty-four hours previously, he looked somewhat surprised. Looking at my notes he said, 'Well, we'll have to wait and see what happens.'

'But can't you do something?' I asked, 'I can't just lie around here for days waiting.'

'We could break the waters if you like,' he volunteered.

'Anything,' I said.

So, at 9.30 am the waters were broken, Paul summoned, and Hannah born shortly before 11 am. She proved to be the opposite of her brother. I was not to see her with her eyes open in the five days of our stay, nor was I able to wake her to feed her. She was, nevertheless, healthy and beautiful, and to our great relief she slept regularly for three and four hours, day and night, for three months, with hardly a single cry.

Yet, even in the midst of life with a new-born baby it was impossible to remain isolated from life outside. In February itself, the ruling Hungarian Socialist Workers' Party decided to accept a multi-party system and also declared the 1956 revolution (always officially referred to as a counter-revolution), to be a popular uprising. I wondered what Miklós would make of it all – he was now in Bloomington, Indiana, and would not return until the summer. His letters were more concerned with his ability to overcome the culture gap he felt in America, and his lack of adequate finances.

We too became infected with the atmosphere of anticipation and excitement. It was now almost seven years since we had arrived in Hungary, intending at that time to stay for just one, or maybe two years. Since then we had renewed our residents' permits every summer, but the birth of the children had put a time limit on our stay. We had decided they should go to school in England and avoid the inevitable Marxist-Leninist teaching combined with compulsory Russian lessons, which left almost everyone we knew unable to ask for a cup of coffee after eight or more years' instruction. We also did not relish the prospect of flat-hunting again, and Ági and Kazi would be returning in the summer for good.

Many of our conversations during walks in the City Park were concentrated on the various possibilities for our future. Laurence's mother had offered to look out for suitable jobs for Paul, but somehow the urgency of the situation seemed to be diminishing with each new development in Hungary's history. On one such walk, we found ourselves behind the rostrum on Dózsa György Street where the party officials would stand on such occasions as the May Day parade. We suddenly noticed that a black star had been sprayed on the edifice, with the word *Vigyázz!* 'Beware!' underneath. There was a policeman standing on guard next to the structure, and nearby we also saw that the statue of Lenin had been shrouded in swathes of plastic sheeting. Not many weeks later the statue was silently, and unceremoniously, removed.

Back in our flat we found ourselves watching the removal of something else – the Chimneysweep. Its crumbling walls were being demolished, the green trelliswork a pile of splintered timber among the broken tiles and dust-covered bricks.

It was June and an announcement was made that Russian was no longer to be a compulsory subject at school. But what was greeted with unbelieving enthusiasm was the news that Imre Nagy was to be reburied at a huge ceremony at which all those executed after '56 would also be commemorated. Now, on our walks in the park, we watched as the facades of the two art galleries and the pillars of Heroes' Square were draped in black cloth. We thought back to Miklós's first visit to England in 1979 when he had acquired a book about Imre Nagy in London, a thick tome he had read from cover to cover but did not risk taking back to Hungary in his suitcase. The date, 1956, and the name Imre Nagy could then only be whispered among friends. Now, booklets were being printed with the list of names of all those who had been sentenced to death, and June 16th – the anniversary of Nagy's execution – was named as the day for the commemoration. There was no doubt in anyone's mind that this was the final step, the point of no return. The tempo of change had been accelerating, every aspect of life felt as though it were in a state of flux, stability was being swept away and we were being swept along with it.

I was awoken by Hannah in the cold hours before dawn on the 16th. I walked over to the window gently rocking her to sleep. Outside, the night was still dark and starry. Below me lay the empty space that had been the Chimneysweep, a few bricks and windblown newspapers all that remained. Just beyond lay Heroes' Square, shrouded in black, awaiting the momentous day which lay ahead, and not much further away was Garay Square, the cats fed and sleeping on the roofs of the silent market. Only at Rákóczi Square would some girls be waiting on the corner, while the all-night tram occasionally rumbled its way past.

The whole city, the whole country, was slumbering its last, unknowing, dreamless and innocent sleep.

Epilogue

Miklós left Lingua to start a new venture of his own and to do his doctorate in American literature. He still has his flat on Rákóczi Square and can regularly be seen shopping at the market.

János still runs Lingua, now in new premises near Margaret Bridge.

Endre and Kati got divorced. Endre later remarried and both lives and works near Lake Balaton.

Feri, Paul's student from the Bükk mountains, left the Music Academy and spent ten years in Iceland. Tamás plays the violin in one of Hungary's best string orchestras, while Zoli finally settled in Switzerland and plays the cello in the Zürich Symphony Orchestra.

Attila abandoned horse and cart jaunts for German tourists, but still rides, and is a well-known figure in Zsámbék where he now lives.

Laurence worked for Andrew Lloyd-Webber for several years. He subsequently wrote his own successful musical on the life of Marlene Dietrich and now works freelance in England.

Geoff took a degree in English and Russian, going on to teach English in numerous places, and is now working on his Ph.D. in linguistics.

Ági and Kazi returned from Belgium to begin new careers: Kazi in the car business, Ági in Management Consultancy.

Cili and Laci moved out of their minuscule flat to a larger one in a neighbouring street. Sadly, Marietta-néni has since died.

Danielle went on to start a degree in Hungarian at London University, though following her marriage – to a man with a Hungarian father – and the happy arrival of two children, she was unable to finish it.

John and Hannah went to the local nursery school where they learnt their first words of Hungarian, and are now at a Hungarian primary school. They are, happily, both bi-lingual and bi-cultural.

Twenty years after first coming to Hungary we are still here. Laurence's claim that Budapest life was 'habit-forming' seems to have been vindicated. We could not then have foreseen what effect Hungary's transition to a new world would have on our lives, the further moves we would make or the new characters we would meet.

That could provide material for a sequel to this book...

Second edition 1999 by
MÁGUS PUBLISHING LTD
1055 Budapest, Balassi B. u. 25. Hungary
Tel./fax: (36) 1 353 45 42
E-mail: magus-vario@mail.matav.hu
Printed in Hungary: Printer Art
ISBN 963 8278 55 2